T0197436

Testimonials

"Cathy Jameson is an industry pioneer and leader in the development of management training for professionals. I have known Cathy personally for many years, and no one understands how to manage a team better. Every member of an organization can benefit from her expertise, whether by learning how to create a healthy work environment or how to improve employee and customer satisfaction. Cathy can help teams be more engaged, more fulfilled, more productive, and ultimately more successful."

Michele Penrose
Director of Global Professional Relations
Henry Schein, Inc.

"I have been working with Cathy Jameson for more than twenty years. She has helped me grow and expand my business during this time. She has incredible strategies for stress reduction and for coping with the daily, weekly, and monthly challenges of running a business. Her skills in delivering the information are key and will motivate you to achieve and accomplish success and growth. Thank you, Cathy, for your dedication to helping others. Through your guidance, I have been able to continually expand and grow whilst coping with the immediate demands of running a business."

Dr. Linda Greenwall
Founder and Owner of Hamstead Health Care
Founder of Dental Wellness Trust, a Charitable Trust in South Africa
London, England

"One of the most important and too often overlooked areas of life is a healthy work environment. Cathy Jameson taught me and my team why and how to create that kind of a healthy environment, and that is why I have a super team that has functioned as a cohesive family for thirty, twenty-two, and seventeen years. We love working together. Cathy, you're a superstar."

Dr. Larry Rosenthal
Founder of the Rosenthal APA Group
Cosmetic Dentistry NYC and Aesthetic Advantage at New York University
New York, New York

"Knowing Cathy Jameson for twenty years, I have seen her work centered upon creating a healthy work environment for thousands of people. She is truly an expert in the field."

Darrell Cain, CPA
Founder of Cain Watters and Associates, a CPA firm
Dallas, Texas

"Over the decades that Cathy and I have known each other, we have had many conversations about leadership and healthy, vital organizations. Cathy believes that an organization can foster a culture that causes it to be high achieving, personally rewarding, and professionally stimulating. I agree. This book can help you create this type of environment in your organization, whether or not you have management responsibilities. Leaders are found at every level of an organization. Become a better leader in your area of influence through embracing the ideas found in *Creating a Healthy Work Environment.*"

Kirk A. Jewell
President
Oklahoma State University Foundation
Stillwater, Oklahoma

"Can you imagine what could happen if you opened your mind and your heart to absorb words of wisdom from a master educator? Today is your day! Dr. Cathy Jameson has repeatedly inspired, fired up, redirected, liberated, and motivated our team. I can't imagine where my business would be today without her loving leadership and guidance."

Dr. Mark Hyman
Author, Speaker, and Television Personality
Greensboro, North Carolina

"Dr. Jameson understands the little-known workplace secret: employees want to work where they are celebrated and appreciated! She has decades of coaching/facilitation experience and can help organizations have their associates sincerely caring for one another—without sacrificing productivity, time management, or team goals. She is an ambassador of positive cultures where all people can thrive."

Craig Clemons
Vice President of Public Relations and Business Development
Express Employment Professionals
Oklahoma City, Oklahoma

"Stress in the workplace can demotivate you, affect your professional and personal relationships, and deteriorate your overall health and well-being. Alleviating chronic stress or finding ways to control or manage it is critical for optimal performance at work and home. Cathy Jameson is an expert in creating healthy, stress-free work environments. She has been doing this successfully for many years. Her expertise shared in this new book is a guide to a brighter, happier, healthier daily work experience. If you are ready to address your stress, then Cathy has the answers to build a new foundation that supports productivity."

Dr. Jill Wade
Founder and CEO of Relevance Total Health
Frisco, Texas

"If you would ask me about the definition of positive energy, my answer would be Dr. Cathy Jameson. She is one of the most constructive and creative people I know. She constantly looks for solutions, even in worst-case scenarios. Her ability to combine the discipline and love of work is inspiring. When I wrote my best-selling book, *The Science and Art of Porcelain Laminate Veneers*, I asked Cathy to write the chapter on management. We were aware of the importance of management in the workplace and the power that would create with the synergy between team members and with clients/patients. With her latest book, *Creating a Healthy Work Environment*, she will touch many people and create a great impact on the professional, emotional, and daily lives of the readers."

Dr. Galip Gurel
Founder and Honorary President of EDAD: Turkish Academy of Aesthetic Dentistry
Editor-in-Chief of Quintessence International (Turkey)
Istanbul, Turkey

"I've known Cathy Jameson for the past twenty-five years. She has worked endlessly over the years along with her husband, Dr. John Jameson, and their team to establish one of the top practice management consulting firms in dentistry. Cathy loves what she does and delivers her messages with knowledge, passion, and energy. She sees the big picture and all the moving parts of a successful practice from the team's view, from the dental spouse's view, and as a consultant to hundreds of practices. Some may view her as my competitor. I view Cathy as a friend and colleague."

Linda Miles, CSP, CMC
Founder, Linda Miles and Associates
Founder, Speaking Consulting Network
Cofounder, Oral Cancer Cause
Virginia Beach, Virginia

Also by Cathy Jameson, PhD

Books
Cosmetic Dentistry Workbook
Great Communication Equals Great Production, 1st and 2nd Editions
Collect What You Produce, 1st and 2nd Editions
Success Strategies, coauthored with Dr. Linda Greenwall

Audio Programs
Star Gazing: Building a 5 Star Team
Great Communication Equals Great Production
Scheduling for Productivity, Profitability, and Stress Control

Video Programs
Keys to Controlling Stress

Other ways to connect and learn more:
Digital Leadership Online Course
Day at a Glance Calendar of Quotes from Cathy's Writing
Inspirational Cards for Every Day

Cathy would like to invite you to join her
on her blog: cathyjameson.com

CREATING
a Healthy Work Environment

Cathy Jameson Ph.D.

www.cathyjameson.com
Cover design and original artwork: Rachel Leslie, Polka Square Design
Coeditors: Sue and John Morris of Editide, Marshfield, Vermont
Photograph of Dr. Jameson for back cover and inside back cover: Gabriel Ceballos, San Francisco, CA
Makeup: Anna Campofiorito, San Francisco, CA
Hair: Scott Bond of Bond Street Hair, New York City
Smile Makeover by Dr. Ken Hamlett of Dallas, Texas

Balboa Press books may be ordered through booksellers or by contacting:

Balboa Press
A Division of Hay House
1663 Liberty Drive
Bloomington, IN 47403
www.balboapress.com
1 (877) 407-4847

Print information available on the last page.

ISBN: 978-1-5043-5325-0 (sc)
ISBN: 978-1-5043-5327-4 (hc)
ISBN: 978-1-5043-5326-7 (e)

Library of Congress Control Number: 2016904101

Balboa Press rev. date: 9/22/2016

To my beloved husband, John:
This book reflects the principles of leadership, honor, and love that you epitomize every day in your work, your community, and your home. You make every environment you touch a bit healthier.
With love and devotion, know that I am grateful.

Cathy

CONTENTS

ACKNOWLEDGMENTS

Each of us is a teacher. We teach ourselves, our children, friends, colleagues, employees, clients, patients, and each person with whom we have an encounter. In the teaching, we learn. Our own lives are enriched when we provide a path of growth for others.

I have been blessed with teachers throughout my life; parents, grandparents, siblings, husband, children, instructors, coaches, schoolteachers, piano teachers, cowboys, horsemen and women, ministers, spiritual leaders, psychologists, and each person I have loved.

During my doctoral study in applied management and decision sciences, I focused my work on leadership and organizational change. My study, research, and academic development at Walden University enhanced my life. That research and my experiences are at the core of this book. When I think about the many people who have affected my life and career, I am humbled and grateful. I dedicate this book to the people who have chosen to be *on purpose* by teaching and inspiring students to be more than they ever imagined possible.

This book has been in my soul for a long time. It has been begging to come out. I have learned through academic study, work experiences, teachers, and life. This book is an amalgamation of these lessons. Its time has come.

My purpose is to make a positive difference in the lives of people in the workplace.

My mission is to be a committed teacher of proven ways to create a healthy work environment where people can thrive in their chosen careers. My instruction will provide a pathway to a culture where people can be creative, make a difference, and spend quality time with people they care about in a fun and nurturing manner.

My vision is to see the work environment become an enriching part of a fulfilled life. I am a teacher, and I am proud to educate. I dedicate this book to all teachers. I know that when I am teaching, I am *on purpose.*

PREFACE

In this book, *Creating a Healthy Work Environment,* we will explore the parameters of transformational leadership. We will delve into the individual principles of this powerful and relevant style of leadership in detail.

I am a teacher and will follow good teaching protocols: Each chapter will include:

1. The theory or principles behind the recommendations
2. The instruction or the how-tos
3. Life examples that you can relate to and transfer to your situation
4. Practice exercises, questions, and exercises that will help you integrate the learning into your life or organization. I call these *creative opportunities* to carry through the concept of "creating," which is at the heart of this book.

With this proven teaching method, I will give you the road map, the guidance, and the experiences to create a healthy work environment.

Let me make a strong point here. This book is written not just for owners, executives, and doctors. This book is written for every person on the team or in the employ of an organization. Each of you makes up the organization, and you have more choices than you may imagine. In your role or position, you can have a positive, constructive effect upon every interaction and on the organization as a whole. Do not discount yourself. You are absolutely fantastic—and your organization cannot function fully and completely without you. However, each of you must accept your responsibility as a leader and make a commitment to yourself and to others to be an asset. The choice is yours. Be "the right person on the bus" (Collins, 2006).

So here we go on a creative journey to a healthy workplace where we can make a difference, serve our purposes, and find joy and fulfillment in our chosen fields. Enjoy!

PART I

THE THEORY: THE FOUNDATION FOR A HEALTHY WORK ENVIRONMENT

The Theory

I am going to lead you through a synopsis of the theory—the research—behind the book you are preparing to read and study. *What! Gasp! Theory?* Yes, theory. The background. The foundation. The reason behind what I am getting ready to teach you. I don't want you to build a work environment on sand! Nope! I want you to build it on rock. Solid rock. And that's the research. The history. The foundations of truth are instrumental for any long-lasting business, relationship, or country.

As a longtime student of piano, I studied theory ad nauseam. I did my "dozen-a-day" and Czerny exercises every day. My first piano recital piece was "The Country Capers." But, lo and behold, after years of intentional study of the theory and many hours of practice, my senior recital piece was Grieg's "Sonata OP. 7," which I can still play. When you truly learn something, you own it. It isn't a fleeting discovery or a passing fancy. It is grounded. Internally yours. You never know how far you can go with a foundation of theory and a lot of practice!

My intention is to provide the theoretical groundwork—the foundation—to give you the mechanisms to turn principles and theory into daily realities: things you can sink your teeth into, make happen, and put into action. *Fair enough?* Okay, then, read on.

GRIEG

CHAPTER 2

Transactional versus Transformational Leadership

Leadership is a function of knowing yourself, having a vision that is well communicated, building trust among colleagues, and taking effective action to realize your own leadership potential.
—Warren Bennis

There are two distinct types of leadership that are evident in the workplace: transactional and transformational. Let's look at each.

Transactional Leadership

Transactional leadership has been dominant in the workplace historically, but this is changing. In this type of work environment, the leader dictates to followers what they will do and how they will do it. The leader indicates requirements and the results that are to be accomplished and outlines the rewards for fulfilling these requirements. There is little interactive communication. Creativity is not encouraged. Rewards are defined by money—not fulfillment or growth. Rewards for work well done are finite. There's not much room for personal development.

Transactional leadership is a hierarchical style of leadership with a top-down style of authority. The employees do not participate in decision making, and their ideas are not encouraged. Communication channels between executives and employees are limited.

Wow! That doesn't sound fun, does it?

Talented people will leave an organization if they are not challenged and appreciated. In a work environment where transactional leadership is evident, attracting and retaining top team members is tough! They may come, but they may not stay.

Certainly, there are times and situations where the executive team or owners must take charge and, of course, they expect and require certain levels of performance. There are times when transactional leadership is not only desired; it is necessary. However, the methods by which leaders encourage productive performance are changing.

Transformational Leadership

In contrast, transformational leaders inspire and motivate employees to achieve excellent results in their work and to become leaders themselves. Their leadership style is horizontal rather than hierarchical. Workers are empowered, and individual goals as well as organizational goals are aligned with their unique talents and abilities.

> The function of leadership is to produce
> more leaders, not more followers.
> —Ralph Nader

Transformational leaders consistently stimulate awareness of the mission and vision of the organization. They encourage team members to be a part of writing goals and designing action plans to accomplish them. In other words, team members participate—and love it.

My Own Survey

In my doctoral research, I performed a survey of three thousand people in the workplace. Participants held various positions of responsibility from the CEO to the newest hires. One of the questions on the survey was, "Do you know the goals of your organization?" Not one person said yes. Another question asked, "Do you have a system of goal setting and goal accomplishment in your organization?" Again, as you would imagine, the answer was no—three thousand nos!

So study the theory and practice!

Transformational leaders are role models. Colleagues and employees respect them. They trust them to do what they say they will do. Followers believe in their leaders, want to be like them, make them proud by performing well, and emulate the lives of these revered leaders. These leaders function not from a place of power but from a place of integrity and nurturing (Bass and Avolio, 1994). Talented people can and will perform excellently when provided education, development opportunities, and feedback, so continuing education is offered. It is not seen as a mandate but as a benefit. A transformational leader sees employees as individual human beings who have lives outside the organization and honor the "whole person." These leaders have a sense of hope and *optimism*.

When transformational leaders set their goals and expectations at a high level, employees tend to do the same thing. Alignment with the purpose, mission, and vision is evident in every aspect of the business. All people, all products, all marketing, and all interactions with clients send the same message. When the leader sets this tone and consistently represents this vision, other members of the team will be more likely to do the same (Jameson, 2000).

Optimism is a belief in and expectation of positive outcomes,
even in the face of difficulty, challenge, or crisis.
Optimism is the expectation for the best in
everybody, everything, and every situation.

People come to an organization and stay committed to the organization for different reasons.

1. Some love the work itself because it gives them a chance to make a difference, affect the life of another, or work toward positive social change.
2. Some want and need the money, the benefits, and the practical, essential elements of life.
3. Some want the social interaction with people who share a common interest and vision.
4. Some thrive in an environment where their gifts and talents are appreciated
5. And some come for all of the above reasons (L. Murphy, 2005).

Rather than coming to work for the sole purpose of drawing a paycheck, people who are inspired and motivated by a transformational leader want to be there. They perform well as a commitment to the organization and the leaders rather than from a posture of compliance. When people find creative expression in their work and experience joy and happiness in the workplace, the emotions transfer to home and family (Bass and Avolio, 1994). Employees today want to be trusted with the freedom to make decisions and to be creative while doing so (Webb, 2007).

What an exciting time in the workplace today. Natural, caring relationships are desired rather than tyrannical relationships that are difficult for all parties. Transformational leadership is the way of the future—and the future is now.

CHAPTER 3

Enlightened Leadership

Enlightened leadership is spiritual if we understand
spirituality not as some kind of religious dogma or ideology
but as the domain of awareness where we experience values
like truth, goodness, beauty, love and compassion, and
also intuition, creativity, insight and focused attention.
—Deepak Chopra

Consider the values that Chopra states in this opening quote: truth, goodness, beauty, love, compassion, intuition, creativity, insight, and focused attention. Interpret those values into your own thought processes and experiences. What does each mean to you? To your organization? Does this seem "fluffy" to you? Something you want to avoid like the plague? Would it be interesting or great if these values were present in your interactions with each other and with your customers?

Throughout this book, I am going to take these fluffy areas and give you nuts and bolts ways to create an environment where this is not only the standard but the norm. People in the digital and technological era of today are not the same as people from the industrial era. Don't turn your head away and pretend you don't see. Embrace the terrific evolution that is occurring as transformational leadership comes into its own. While the great leaders, theorists, and researchers have professed the values of this type of leadership for centuries, its time has come.

Today's knowledge worker wants to maximize potential, find satisfaction in the workplace, and be respected by colleagues and employers. They want to be competent in their jobs. People spend so much time at work, and they want to enjoy being there. With a more respectful, communicative relationship between employer and employee, the employer/leader becomes the one who serves the employee rather than the reverse (Durkheim, 1961).

The first responsibility of a leader is to define reality.
The last is to say thank you.
In between, the leader is a servant.
—Max De Pree

Hierarchy of Needs

Can a book be written on management without including a nod of the head to Maslow? Not this psychologist! The work of Abraham Maslow is foundational to the principles being described throughout this book.

Maslow (1999) developed a hierarchy of needs, delineating the various levels of need in a human being that must be satisfied for a person to rise to the next level of development. People can advance to the next level of need only when they have satisfied the previous level or levels. This principle applies to the work environment and life in general. The hierarchy of needs (Maslow, 1999) follows (from lowest to highest):

1. physiological needs
2. safety and security needs
3. social needs: love and belonging
4. esteem needs
5. self-actualization

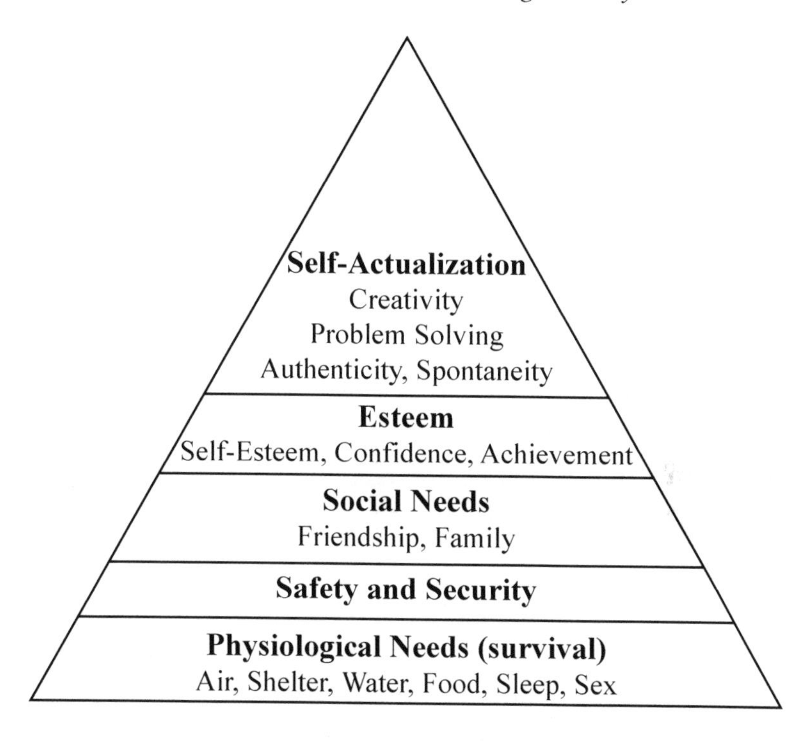

Maslow's Hierarchy of Needs.

In an environment that professes and practices what Maslow termed *enlightened management* (1998), employees are trusted, and they trust the leaders. Needs are identified, and effort is made to satisfy those needs. Mutual care and respect are evident between and among employees and employers. In this kind of an enlightened environment, the concept of teamwork, cooperation, and spirit of unity can develop. Synergy is desired. Well-established systems make it possible for people to function at an optimum level, synergistically.

A young person with whom I work said, "I know I can do what I'm supposed to do because I can count on my teammates to do what they are supposed to do. We function like a well-oiled machine: no glitches. Things flow really well because we are a cohesive unit. It's fun!" Unselfish behavior is the hallmark rather than a competitive, hostile environment.

Flow

Csikszentmihalyi (1990) described *flow* as "a state in which people are so involved in an activity that nothing else seems to matter; the experience itself is so enjoyable that people will do it even at great cost, for the sheer sake of doing it." This kind of experience, inside or outside of work, is pleasurable to the point that people lose track of time and are not easily distracted from the activity in which they are engaged. They are deeply involved in the activity and do not want to stop—even for meals. They may find it difficult to turn their attention to other activities or to other people; time seems to pass quickly without notice (Csikszentmihalyi, Rathunde, and Whalen, 1993).

Csikszentmihalyi and his colleagues found that flow is being in a zone or a mental state where people become so fully immersed in an activity or project that they have focused energy, total involvement, and enjoyment in what they are doing. Flow is "completely focused motivation." People who truly love their work and the service they are providing are happier, more successful, and accomplish a higher level of performance. The flow theory proposes three conditions that have to be met to create a state of flow:

1. A clear set of goals and methods for evaluation. This provides directions and structure to tasks being performed.
2. Clear and immediate feedback that allows for rapid adjustments to be made to improve performance
3. A balance between the *perception* of the difficulty of the task and the perception of the ability to perform the task. Confidence is a characteristic of flow. (Csikszentmihalyi, 1990)

The challenges of staying in flow are boredom, apathy, and anxiety.

1. Boredom: Challenges are few and far between; a person's skills level exceeds the requirement of the job; talent is not nurtured. Remedy: *These people will seek other opportunities if they are not challenged. Provide new responsibilities that give them a chance to stretch and grow. Trust them.*
2. Apathy: No interest. Skills are underused. Challenges are low. Unmotivated. Don't care. Remedy: *Find their interest. Match the interests to the tasks. Light the fire.*
3. Anxiety: Challenges are so high that they exceed a person's ability or skill level. This causes distress and discomfort. Remedy: *New skills can be learned. Provide support, education, and feedback to lift skill level and confidence.*

Flow can be discovered and enjoyed in the workplace. Step out of your comfort zone. Stretch. Find flow right where you are. Don't depend on anyone else. Take responsibility for your own pursuit of happiness.

> Our deepest fear is not that we are inadequate. Our deepest fear is that we are powerful beyond measure. It is our Light, not our Darkness, that most frightens us. You are a child of God. Your playing small does not serve the world. There is nothing enlightened about shrinking so that other people won't feel insecure around you. We were born to manifest the glory of God that is within us.
>
> —Marianne Williamson

PART II

THE ACTION PLAN: HOW TO CREATE A HEALTHY WORK ENVIRONMENT

CHAPTER 4

The Right Team Members

Good teams become great ones when the members trust each other enough to surrender the *me* for the *we*.
—Phil Jackson

The most important asset of an organization is its people. The people produce the product, nurture clients, represent the organization, and make success possible. Salaries and benefits are usually the highest overhead item. This is an investment that benefits clients, the organization, and the owners/executives. Is there a better place to invest?

If you consider salaries and benefits for employees to be a cost rather than an investment, you may have the wrong people on your team. Or perhaps talent has been left under a basket and has not been given a chance to shine. "You are the light of the world. A city set on a hill cannot be hidden; nor does anyone light a lamp and put it under a basket, but on the lampstand, and it gives light to all who are in the house" (Matthew 5:14).

If you have the right team members, you will agree that this overhead item is an investment! And a good one. One that will come back to you multifold.

The Right People on the Bus

In *Good to Great,* Jim Collins reported that "getting the right people on the bus" is the factor that distinguishes a good organization from a great one. Collins (2001) noted, "We thought that people were a company's greatest asset. We were wrong. The *right* people are a company's greatest asset." Collins and his team of researchers found that great organizations "got the right people on the bus. Got the wrong people off the bus. And got the right people in the right seats." I would respectfully add doing the right things in the right way.

Creating a work environment that attracts the right people, nurtures these people to be productive, and keeps them throughout time is not easy, but it is worth the effort.

> As a leader, working to develop and support my team is one of my greatest joys and one of the most productive things I do.
> —Dr. Chuck Puntillo

How does a leader/owner get the right people on the bus? The first step is to hire correctly. Easily said. Not easily done. Hire slowly and hire correctly. Turnover of a quality team member is costly—emotionally and financially—but it happens. People may leave your business due to personal circumstances, and those positions will need to be filled. If your organization is growing, new positions may need to be established.

The following are the steps of a healthy hiring process:

1. Prepare before you start the search.
2. Determine the characteristics or skills you wish the new person to possess.
3. Write (or review) the written job description.
4. Make sure it is appropriate and current for the position you are filling or creating.
5. Describe the attitude and personality you desire.

6. Hire characteristics and attitude first. You can always teach (or accelerate) the skills.

> Nothing can stop a person with the right attitude
> from *achieving a goal.* Nothing on earth can
> help the person with the wrong attitude.
> —Thomas Jefferson

Once you have determined the characteristics and attitude of the desired new employee, analyze the description of the position (the job description). This should contain what the person is to do and the expected end results of their performance (the performance objectives).

1. Sources of potential candidates
    a. Personnel agencies, employment recruiters, talent scouts. If you are using a hiring service to assist you, they will provide necessary information for you—and will gather appropriate information from you. Depending on what you want, they can access candidates and do all pre- and post-hiring requirements, including negotiation of compensation.
    b. Internet sources
    c. Social media
    d. Associations related to your profession
    e. Colleagues of your own employees
    f. Great clients, customers, or patients
    g. Schools of your profession, colleges, universities, job fairs, vocational schools, and technical schools
    h. Newspapers, magazines, newsletters, blogs, etc.

If you are posting an advertisement for the position, carefully construct your ad or hire a professional to assist you. Your ad needs to "sell" potential candidates on the benefits of your company and the position, but you need to be clear about expectations of the position; otherwise, you are wasting your time.

Administrative and Marketing Assistant

Seeking a customer-service oriented administrative assistant for a growing and diverse organization. This key role will provide administrative, marketing, and sales support to the entire team. Must be willing to work in a fast-paced and fun environment. Candidate must be resourceful, self-motivated, and have strong verbal and written communication skills, excel in spelling and grammar, have a positive team attitude, and have the work ethic to be productive while working unsupervised. The successful candidate will have 3+ years of previous administrative experience, or a four-year college degree, computer proficient with solid knowledge of MS Office (Word/Excel), PowerPoint, and Outlook. Sales, marketing, and graphic design ability is a plus. Ability to multitask is required. Minimal travel is required to fulfill job responsibilities. Please e-mail your cover letter, resume, and referrals in Word format to ABC@XYZ.com

2. If you are performing the hiring process yourself, do the following:
   a. Ask interested candidates to send a resume and a letter of introduction to an e-mail address or to your business address, if that is acceptable to you.
   b. Review all resumes and letters. Analyze carefully. Look for relevant information to your company and to the position, but also pay close attention to the diligence with which the candidate prepared the resume and letter. In addition to the technical aspects of the documents, look for accuracy, clarity, neatness, and care.

c. Contact all candidates. To those who are not going to be invited for an interview, send a letter thanking them for their interest and telling them the position is not available at this time. For those parties you wish to interview, contact them and invite them in for an interview. This interview can be with a manager, supervisor, or owner, depending on the size of your organization and the personnel situation. While you have them on the phone, ask a predetermined set of questions. Not too many. But, you want to compare answers from one candidate to the other and hear their phone voice. In addition, you want to see if they can think on their feet and speak well. Then invite them into the office for a face-to-face interview, unless they perform so poorly on the phone interview that you know they are not right for the job; if not, send them a regret letter. You may want to consider a video call for the initial interview.
d. When the candidate arrives, ask them to complete a handwritten application. Follow all the regulations of your state or country. Get applications from your own HR division or from a professional HR company.
e. In your interview, ask open-ended questions. Pay close attention to how the candidates present themselves. How are they groomed and dressed? Do they look like they care? Do they look appropriate for the position? Are they confident, well spoken, and courteous? Does their personality seem to fit into your corporate/company culture? You should do about 30 percent of the talking, and the candidate should do about 70 percent of the talking. Ask for permission to take notes. Review what you are looking for and ask what the candidate is seeking. Go over any pertinent details.

f. Invite your top two or three candidates (or more, if appropriate) back for a second interview. Arrange for background checks and contact all references. Do not fail to contact references. For a small organization, ask team members to participate in the second interview. It is important that the candidate fit in. This interview will be longer and more comprehensive. Review the job description in detail. Again, make sure that you and the candidate are seeking the same thing. Review the compensation package as well as any other data relevant to the position.

g. Make your decision and contact the candidate being invited to join you. Offer the position. For any candidates who you are not going to hire, send a letter thanking them and telling them that you will keep their resume in case another opportunity arises. (If the first candidate does not work out for some reason, you may wish to offer the position to one of the other top candidates)

Once a person is hired, you then move to the Integration phase of their employment.

In Summary: Three Factors to Consider When Hiring

1. Focus on desired results. Determine what you want this person to accomplish. What are the end results that are needed from that person—and from that position? Address these needs during the interview process. Do not ramble through a list of activities, actions, and tasks. Focus on the end results—those that matter most.
2. Study and discuss previous experience. You want to be aware of skills the candidate has acquired and look carefully at how those skills could translate to your business. A person's past experience is valuable, but use careful interviewing and

inquiry to determine if the person is willing and able to adapt to your systems and functions.

3. What is the personality? The attitude? Does it seem this person would fit in your organization? Consider having different people or groups participate in some aspect of the hiring process to see it there is a fit.

My husband, Dr. John Jameson, says this about the right team members:

> The people on my team are critical to the quality of care I consider imperative. They are a direct reflection of me and of my organization. I hire people who have a warm personality, who communicate well, and who are drawn to taking care of people. It's important to me to enjoy every one of my days. And I want to create a work environment where my team members feel the same way. Our happiness with each other and with our work impacts each experience a patient has with our practice.

Having the "right people on the bus" is the driving force for creating a healthy work environment.

Creative Opportunities

1. Review your hiring processes. Do you have a current personnel policy manual? Does it reflect your vision of having a healthy work environment? If there are places where change would be beneficial, make those changes.
2. Review your application form to ensure it follows the guidelines of your state or country. Does it ask the questions that are

important to you? Does it provide the right information to allow you to make qualified decisions?

3. Review the job description and make changes if beneficial. Do the job descriptions detail what a person is supposed to do—and how? Are the goals and expected results clearly identified? Are your expectations clear? If not, alter.
4. When a new person is hired, commit to a spectacular integration phase.

CHAPTER 5

Integration

Synergy means "two heads are better than one." Synergy is the habit of creative cooperation. It is teamwork, open-mindedness, and the adventure of finding new solutions to old problems. But, it doesn't just happen on its own. It is a process and through that process, people bring all their personal experience and expertise to the table. It is the idea that the sum of the whole is greater than the sum of the parts.
—Stephen R. Covey

Once you have hired the right person, spend quality time integrating him/her into the organization and into the responsibilities of the position. No matter how long someone may have worked in your profession or their level of experience, they will not know *your* systems. This does not mean that experience is useless. Not at all. However, every business is unique, and orientation and education will provide a valuable understanding of what you do, how you do it, and why you administer systems in a certain way.

Orientation

Carefully create a training and education plan appropriate to the position. Don't throw someone into the mix and expect him or her to be successful without this. The time you invest in coaching and integration will be profitable. In an environment of respectful orientation, the new person will feel valued and encouraged. His or her energy will reflect your support.

Clear expectations are the foundation of accountability. So clarify! What is the new employee supposed to do? How is each task and system to be administered? Who will do the mentoring? When? What are the expected end results? How will progress be evaluated?

In the first few days of a person's employment, go over the personnel protocols: how and when payroll will be distributed, specifics about the benefit package, hours of work, attire, etc., all of which will be documented in the personnel policy manual. The new employee should sign a statement that he or she has read the manual and agrees to cooperate with the company protocols. Create a personnel file and add it to the other files of all employees. Clarifying these factors is basic to safety, security, and comfort. Excellent orientation and education provides benefits for the new team member.

1. They will become competent and productive more rapidly.
2. They will fit into the team and organization as a whole.
3. They will be more likely to stay.

Remember that turnover is costly. Invest time and money in training and integration.

Education

Once orientation has been completed, initiate the didactic training period by reviewing the specifics of the job description and prioritizing each responsibility. Following the proven steps of adult education, proceed with your training program. Here are those proven steps:

1. Define the expectations and goals to be accomplished.
2. Decide what the person will study first, second, third, etc. Develop a lesson plan.
3. Determine who will provide the coaching for each segment of the lesson plan.
4. Schedule time for instruction.
5. Carefully describe what and how you want each task to be done.
6. Demonstrate.
7. Have them perform the task with you observing and coaching them.
8. Once they have met your approval on an individual task, turn it over to them.
9. Evaluate progress along the way. Don't think that one evaluation is all that will ever be needed. Continuous feedback is appreciated and beneficial for skill mastery.

In fact, give a new employee feedback and coaching every day. Assign a person on the team to be his or her mentor. At the end of each day, the mentor will ask what aspects of work went well and what was difficult or confusing. Delving into those issues quickly will ensure correctness and avoidance of wrong habits. Encourage questions. Good questions indicate an interest in doing things correctly.

Benefits of Mentoring

- Daily mentoring will allow for immediate instruction, feedback, encouragement, and improvement.
- Daily mentoring will lead to confidence as well as competence.
- Daily mentoring will answer any questions that arise.
- Daily mentoring will go a long way to support mastery.

Don't wait until three months have passed to give the new employee a performance review. When something is done well, say so. Solidify results by noticing steps that are taken in the right direction.

Integration

Integrate your new employee as quickly as possible so he or she can move from being an individual worker to a member of a division or department, and then to a fully functioning member of the team and a contributor to the organization.

During this initial phase of employment, make the new person feel welcome. Go to lunch, individually and as a group. Depending on the size and location of your organization, perhaps share a meal at someone's home or at a restaurant. Good things happen when people break bread together! Invite families, if appropriate. You want the family to love the business too! Their support will be valuable.

Have a retreat, luncheon, or special team meeting where you go over the company's vision, mission, goals, and communication avenues or channels. Orientation, education, and integration can make the difference in how readily a person adapts to your culture, how quickly he or she becomes productive, and whether the new employee stays on board with you.

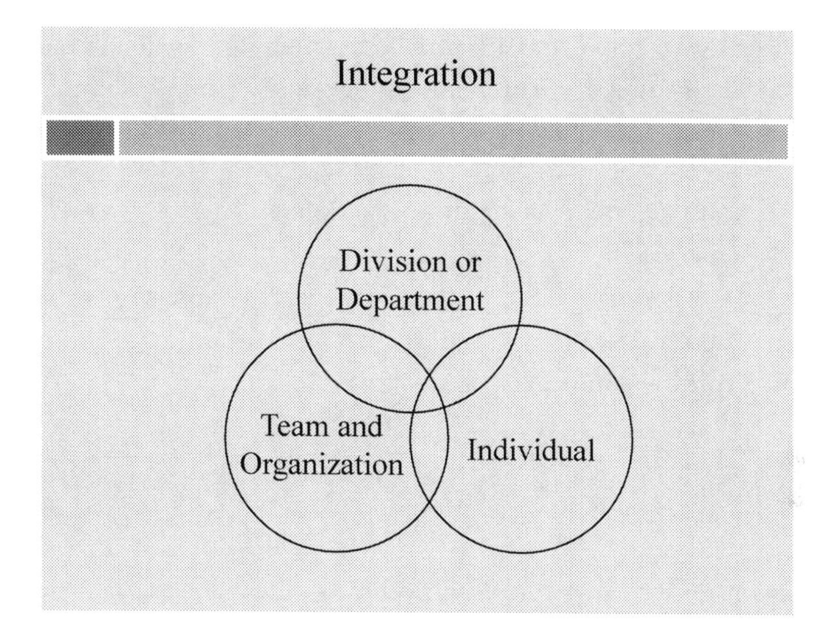

Keeping Those Good Employees—and Keeping Them Happy!

One of the great theorists of motivation in the workplace, Frederick Herzberg, believed that if and when leaders and managers understand motivational factors, employees and the organization benefit from increased productivity and a decrease in the costs that come from rampant turnover (Herzberg, Mausner, and Snyderman, 2007).

Two sets of factors affect an employee's performance. The first set relates to the work environment itself. Herzberg calls these "hygienic" or extrinsic motivators. Extrinsic motivators do not actually stimulate a person toward improved performance. However, if these factors are not stable and acceptable, they become "dissatisfiers" and can deflate a person's performance or cause him or her to leave. These basic needs must be fulfilled or satisfied before a person can move upward in productivity and loyalty (Herzberg et al., 2007).

Usually, an employee's dissatisfaction will occur due to discontent about one (or more) of the following extrinsic factors. Complaints will center on the following issues:

- company policy and administration
- supervision
- interpersonal relations with peers, supervisors, and subordinates
- working conditions
- salary
- status
- job security

Csikszentmihalyi says that having the above entities will not make people happy, but *not* having them will make them unhappy (1990).

The second set of factors includes "intrinsic motivators." They address the issues of job satisfaction and job fulfillment. These factors increase productivity in an employee and promote longevity. These are the factors that *do* promote happiness.

- achievement
- recognition
- interesting and challenging work
- advancement
- responsibility

These two sets of factors or "motivators" go hand in hand to create a healthy work environment. People need rewards, motivation, or challenges to maximize their skills and talents in the workplace (Herzberg et al., 2007). Their hygienic factors—physiological, safety, and security needs—need to be met to move up the ladder or hierarchy of ultimate development (Maslow, 1998). By following the processes I have outlined in this chapter, you will go a long way toward implementing both sets of motivators into the life of a new employee—that "right team member." Once these factors are part of your culture, all people will benefit.

Integration

The time, money, and effort you put into the integration of a new employee will provide a significant return on investment. Give a new team member a chance to be successful through orientation, education, and integration. These three phases are essential parts of creating a healthy work environment.

(See the appendix for a copy of the new employee orientation checklist we use in our company.)

Creative Opportunities

1. Make sure the job description is current and includes tasks, responsibilities, descriptions of how each task is to be completed, and expected goals and end results.
2. Develop a training protocol for new employees (orientation and education).
3. Determine who will provide the training for each task and agree on a time frame for completion of each phase of training. Follow adult-learning principles.
4. Assign a mentor to each new team member. Orient the mentor to his or her role and responsibilities.
5. Give feedback often—both corrective feedback and positive feedback.

CHAPTER 6

Purpose

Purpose is the place where your deep
gladness meets the world's needs.
—Frederick Buechner

The right team members are in place. An excellent job of integration has transpired. An important part of orientation and integration is sharing the purpose, mission, vision, and goals of the organization. You must be clear about that first!

Being *on purpose* is the motivational factor that drives you and your team to provide the services—professionally and personally—that are the core of your business. Your purpose goes deeper than—and will outlast—the technical aspects of your business. The purpose is the "why" behind all that you do. Your purpose is your inspiration—your calling.

Purpose means each of us following a deeper call. It
means living inside the question, "Am I making a living
doing the work that I love to do?" It means being able to
say, "Does my life matter?" When we scratch under the
surface of our drive for making a living, what's there?
—Richard Leider

People don't "buy into" what you do; what matters is why you do it. And although you may feel energized to do something because of money, status, or "making a living," none of that will endure. The ultimate driving force that supports the building of a legacy is the purpose.

Purpose defines the culture of the organization. It goes beyond—or perhaps deeper into—the meaningfulness of work. It's the core. Each person on the team will have a purpose of his or her own. When members of a team find a place where they can pursue their own purposes, they create and exude immeasurable energy. They create healthy work environments.

Being On Purpose

Recently, I was invited to provide a workshop for a group of professionals in Cabo San Lucas. This amazing group of people was on purpose. They exuded a commitment to excellence. They evidenced support rather than competition—even though they worked in the same field.

No one missed a single class despite being in a beautiful place with sun, ocean, and fun (and some participants were coming from ice, snow, and freezing temperatures). They were there to enjoy the location and each other, but—more emphatically—they were there to learn ways to improve their businesses and their lives. They love their chosen profession and are on a path of continuous improvement.

The enthusiasm and commitment were refreshing. Three of the groups worked on the same block in their city. People often asked, "Isn't it weird to work so close to someone who is your direct competition?"

They answered, "Absolutely not. We support each other. We help each other out. We teach each other. We want success for all of us. The better each of us does to elevate our own business, the higher we raise the bar of client expectation—and that helps all of us."

Now, that's healthy! That is how to create healthy relationships and healthy work environments. Jealousy is an unproductive emotion! It subtracts. Camaraderie adds.

Different Types of Work Attitudes

As I have worked with people throughout the United States and around the world, I have seen four specific work types or work attitudes.

Group 1: People who hate work. They come to work for the paycheck and resent every minute. On Monday morning, they are wishing it were Friday. At eight o'clock in the morning, they wish it was five o'clock. On Sunday night, they are dreading Monday and having to go to work. This is the "it's just a job" group—the eight-to-fiver who only works for the paycheck. These people gripe and whine about everything: bosses, clients, coworkers. They stir the pot and blame others for anything that goes wrong. They take no personal responsibility and don't know or care what accountability means! Work is a vehicle to what they want to do when they are not at work. Nothing more. These people are complacent.

Group 2: Work is a necessity. It is part of life. Like the first group, they have to work to make a living, put food on the table, keep a roof over their heads, take care of family, etc. The paycheck and benefits are important, but these people do not dread the work. It's fine. They have a good work ethic and do what they are supposed to do, and they don't gripe about it. However, they lack passion for the work and for the service they are providing. It's part of life—a "have-to" more than a "want-to." These people are compliant.

Group 3: These people have chosen a career path based on something they like to do. They want to pursue work that has meaning and allows them to use their talent or education (or both). These people like their profession and their line of work. They don't resent going to work and want to thrive in a workplace that is healthy, creative, and has a positive culture. They want to make a good living and feel proud about the work they do. These people are dedicated.

Group 4: Here are the people who feel a "calling" for their work. They are paid for the work they do, but they love the work so much that the joy and fulfillment are more important than the money. They want to use their talent for the benefit of others in order to make a difference. They have passion for their work that is evident in their continuous improvement, creativity, and focused effort put forth every day—in every aspect of their work. These people are on purpose and are clear about the "why" of their chosen profession or career. These people are committed.

You may see yourself in one of the four groups—or you may find yourself in more than one at different times, depending on circumstances. There is no such thing as status quo, so you—and the circumstances of your life—will always change and evolve. You may find your "purpose" changes or evolves. Everything we do prepares us for whatever is next. So there's a reason for all situations. "To everything there is a season."

Change is okay. Change is healthy. Be aware of changes occurring within you—and honor them. Remember to listen to that "still, small voice within" and ask yourself relevant questions: "Am I on purpose? Do I feel fulfilled? Am I using my talents? Am I happy? Is this a healthy work environment where I can thrive? If not, what can I do to change it? Can I make a difference in *this* workplace to create health for myself and others?"

Your own happiness—or lack of it—will impact every person in your life: family, loved ones, and colleagues. Honor yourself by finding work that speaks to your spirit. If you have talent that lies within (and everyone does) and you do not express that talent, you will become ill. Your talents and gifts need to "come out," be expressed, and serve a purpose.

A *Course In Miracles* states the following:

> In any situation in which you are uncertain, the first thing to consider, very simply, is "What do I want to come of this? What is it for?" The clarification of the goal belongs at the beginning, for it is this which will determine the outcome. Doubt is the result of conflicting wishes. Be sure of what you want, and doubt becomes impossible. Nothing is difficult that is wholly desired.

Victor Frankl suggested we "let life question us." He suggested that a sense of purpose is not handed to us on a silver platter; rather, we "decide" to have and fulfill our purpose: we choose.

I choose to live by choice, not by chance; to make changes, not excuses; to be motivated, not manipulated; to be useful, not used; to excel, not compete. I choose self-esteem, not self-pity. I choose to listen to my inner voice, not the random opinion of others.

—Rick Warren

When you know who you are, when you integrate your core values into every fiber of your business, when you are clear about your ideal and work toward that, and when you realize that the service you provide is of benefit to others, you discover the *joy* of work. Work based on a clear purpose—the "why"—can be a rewarding and fulfilling facet of your total life, rather than a dreaded necessity. The choice is yours. Choose to be on purpose by creating a healthy work environment.

Creative Opportunities

1. Spend quiet time with yourself. Define your purpose: the purpose of your organization or business and the personal purpose that you are—or want—to serve in your lifetime.
2. Write this down. Remember that this is the "why" of your work—or of your life.
3. If you are the owner of the business, share this purpose with your team. And certainly share this with your new employees—those new team members.
4. Reevaluate your purpose statement from time to time. Life changes. Circumstances change. Make sure that you are clear about your purpose as life evolves for you and as your business grows.
5. Discuss this valuable "heart" of your business with your team. This is your inspiration, your ultimate motivator; your "why."

CHAPTER 7

Mission Statement

Mission statements can help focus the organization on what really matters—to itself as well as to its stakeholders. Mission statements are important to organizations of all types (public, private, not-for-profit, for-profit, family-owned, etc.). A key reason for such importance is the mission statement's guidance of strategic and day-to-day, operational decisions. Additionally, mission statements represent the glue that binds organizations together.
—Duane Ireland and Michael Hitt

What is a *mission statement*? And why do most management experts and business leaders recommend that an organization create and abide by this statement of mission? And if it is so important, why have so few organizations created one?

Let's look at each of these questions and seek answers.

What is a Mission Statement?

The *Business Dictionary* defines a mission statement in the following manner: "a written declaration of an organization's core purpose and focus that normally remains unchanged over time." The dictionary goes on to say, "Properly crafted mission statements (1) serve as filters to separate what is important from what is not,

(2) clearly state which markets will be served and how, and (3) communicate a sense of intended direction to the entire organization."

Simply put, your mission statement (1) states what business you are in; (2) defines the purpose of that business; and (3) forms the first step in a well-defined business plan or strategic plan.

Here are some examples of mission statements:

Microsoft: "At Microsoft, our mission is to enable people and businesses throughout the world to realize their full potential. We consider our mission statement a commitment to our customers."

Amazon: "To be Earth's most customer-centric company where customers can find and discover anything they want to buy online. We endeavor to offer customers the lowest possible prices."

Henry Schein: "To provide innovative, integrated health care products and services and to be trusted advisors and consultants to our customers—enabling them to deliver the best quality patient care and enhance their practice management efficiency and profitability."

Dr. Mark Hyman: "We are a team of compassionate, dedicated professionals who provide optimal dental care using state-of-the-art technology. We are enthusiastic in our commitment to patients, to excellence, and to building relationships within our community."

And here is my personal mission statement for my career:

Cathy Jameson, PhD: "My mission is to be a committed teacher of proven ways to create a healthy work environment where people can thrive in their chosen career. My instruction will provide a pathway to a culture where people can be creative, make a difference, and spend quality time with people they care about in a fun and nurturing manner."

Your Backbone

A mission statement is like the backbone or spine of a company or organization (or a person). When you and your organization make decisions, this is the benchmark or measuring stick. As you consider a decision, ask, "If we do this, will it help us fulfill our ultimate mission?" The answer must be yes. If the answer is not a profound and confident yes, then go back to the drawing board. Either alter your decision—or don't go there! The question and your answer will give you the guidance needed to make decisions that are meaningful and congruent with you and your company.

Why do most management experts and business leaders recommend that an organization create and abide by this statement of mission?

Frances Hesselbein, president and CEO of the Frances Hesselbein Leadership Institute said,

> The leader mobilizes people around the mission for the organization, making it a powerful force in the uncertain times ahead. Coordination around the mission generates a force that transforms the workplace into one in which workers and teams can express themselves in their work and find significance beyond the task, as they manage for the mission.

Every factor that affects the business, team members, and clients must be in alignment. Whether you are hiring a person or designing a product, sales protocol, marketing plan, or management system, all needs to be in alignment. How can you determine if there is alignment? You measure your decisions with the mission statement. Ask yourself, "If we do this, will it help us fulfill our ultimate mission?" Again, the answer must be yes.

Claudio Pannunzio, president of i-Impact Group, Inc. said, "A mission statement is the vehicle that enables you to convey the reasons why your organization exists. A solid mission statement is as important as your business plan, as it explains in a concise and passionate manner the reasons behind your business's existence" (Pannunzio, 2011).

If this is so important, why does this seem so difficult—so neglected?

There are various reasons. Let's look at them.

See No Reason

Remember this truism: all behavior is driven by asking, "What's in this for me?" People or organizations have to see the benefit of any activity before they will do it. If a leader or an organization as a whole does not see the benefit of a mission statement, then the time, effort, and thought processes will not be invested in its creation. For many, this seems too "fluffy!" Many people—business leaders and professionals—are didactic in nature. They ask, "What's the bottom line? Is this worth the effort? What will this do to increase profits?"

If people think they are only coming to work to do something the "boss" wants them to do, but they lack a sense of importance or relevance, motivation wanes. Focus the energies of the team members on a mission that is powerful enough to motivate from within and there is no limit to the level of accomplishment. Increased productivity and profitability are the result (Jameson, 2010).

Peter Drucker said, the fact that a "business mission is so rarely given adequate thought is perhaps the most important single cause of business frustration."

The Council for the Advancement of Small Business and Entrepreneurship at George Washington University found that approximately 85 percent of small- and medium-sized businesses in the Washington metro area that sought their services did not have a mission statement. These researchers stated,

> A small business cannot afford to run without a clearly defined mission. Such misguided functioning may lead to the ultimate failure of the venture. Writing a mission statement is the first strategic decision a small business needs to take. While many excuses are made for not creating a mission statement, our view

> is that such excuses are unfounded and reveal a lack of strategic thought. (Toftoy and Chatterjee, 2014)

Don't Know How

So here are some guidelines. A mission statement has four components:

- Who are you?
- What do you do?
- What is the importance of your work/service?
- The mission statement is empowered by highly emotional words that reflect the values imperative to you and your organization.

Use this worksheet to develop or refine your business or personal mission statement.

Four Aspects of Your Mission Statement

1. Who are you?

   ____

   ____

2. What do you do?

   ____

   ____

3. What is the importance of your work?

   ____

   ____

4. Empowerment: highly emotional words that reflect your values?

   ____

   ____

Values

Start with your values. Your mission statement will include the imperative values that are essential elements of your work and of your organization as a whole. *Webster* defines value as "something that is held up as important. A principle or quality intrinsically valuable or desirable." Synonyms for values are standards, morals, ethics, ideals, principles, and significance.

Think about your organization. Reflect on your purpose: the why of your existence, your reason for being, and the effect you want to have. Think of the values you believe must be honored in every action, interaction, or decision you make.

Now write those down in the space below. You may wish to discuss these as a team. What values are most important? What values do you all agree are imperative? These value words will appear in your mission statement.

Writing the Mission Statement

Step 1: Write down the highly emotional, empowering words that motivate you (values):

____

____

____

Step 2: Write out who you are and what you do—or what business you are in and what service you provide. Include the importance and purpose of that service.

____

____

____

Step 3: Combine the first two steps to create a mission statement. (The leadership team can do this, but I prefer to work on this as a team, if possible)

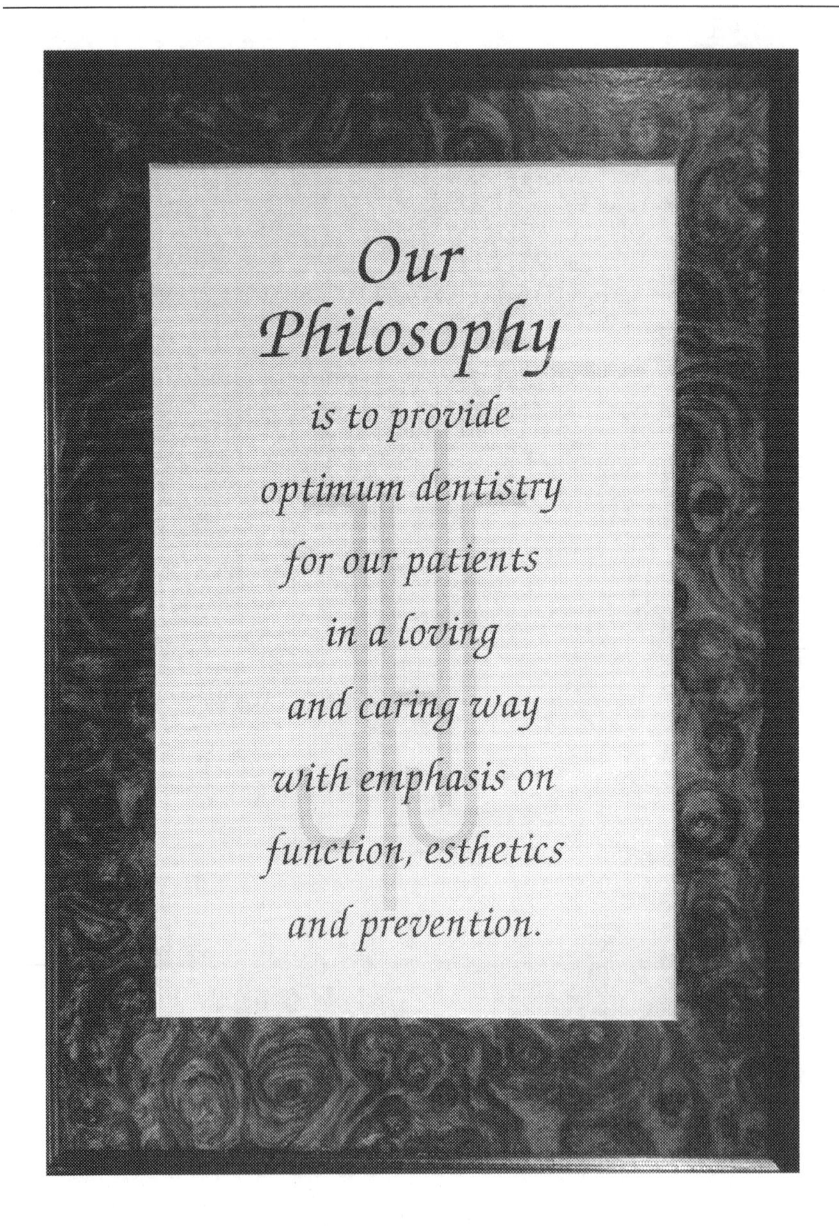

The Mission Statement of John H. Jameson, DDS

Step 4: Prepare the statement for display. Have it written up beautifully. Then matte and frame the mission statement and place it where your clients and team can see it.

Step 5: Read the statement often and keep it in mind as a driving force. Revise it when appropriate.

The Process

Remember the four groups of employees I outlined earlier? You want the fourth group of people on your team. The more engaged and motivated they are, the more productive and profitable your business will be. Perhaps more importantly, your workplace will be more enjoyable and more fulfilling in the long run.

Engage the team in this process. Go through all the exercises I have just given you. Ask for input. Let the most important and most emotionally charged thoughts come to the surface and find their way into your mission statement. Write the first draft, let people reflect on it, and adjust as appropriate. Write the final statement. Ask for a commitment from each team member to support and epitomize the mission of your organization.

Placing the mission statement where clients, customers, and team members can see it serves as a continuous reminder of the company's mandate to ensure that each activity, action, and word spoken aligns with its mission.

A mission statement and the process of creating this benchmark for the organization is a foundational part of creating a healthy work environment.

Creative Opportunities

1. Go through the exercises in this chapter. Do this alone or as a team. Even if you choose to do this alone, bring the information to the team for discussion.
2. If you are the owner, you may have created your own mission statement. That is fine, but bring this to your team for evaluation, contemplation, and alteration (if necessary).
3. You may choose to do this as an exercise with the entire team and create a mission statement that you all believe reflects who you are and what you do and is supported by highly emotional words that express the values that are imperative to you.
4. Have your mission statement matted and framed and placed where you and your clients can see it. As you are making decisions, always ask, "If we do this, will it help us to fulfill our ultimate mission?" Remember that the answer must be yes. If not, go back to the drawing board.

CHAPTER 8

Vision

Leadership is the capacity to translate vision into reality.
—Warren Bennis

Vision

Although the mission statement is your benchmark, the development of a vision moves you toward greater clarity of what you specifically want in your work and workplace. What do you see as your "ideal" workplace? Focus on the ideal. Why not? Proverbs 23:7 says, "As a man thinketh in his heart, so is he." Napoleon Hill stated, "Whatever the mind of man can conceive and believe, so shall he achieve." And Earl Nightingale stated simply and profoundly, "We become what we think about."

Vision differs from mission in that it is focused on the future. The things you focus upon become your reality. So focus on the things you want. When you focus on the things you want—that which you sincerely and passionately desire—these things come to pass.

Apply this to your design of your healthy work environment. What do you consider the ideal? Whatever you consider the ideal, focus upon that. There is no reason to accept anything less than your ideal, whatever that is to you.

Your first step is defining what *ideal* means to you. What you determine to be ideal is uniquely yours. Looking deep within yourself and being true to your unique vision is the beginning of your strategic plan. It is the pathway to abundant success.

Remember that each person has the ability to impact his or her work environment. Don't underestimate your influence as a leader in your organization.

Here are some important questions to consider as you develop your vision—the future focus of your healthy work environment:

- What kind of service do you want to provide?
- How do you want to provide that service?
- What do you want your clients/customers/patients to experience each time they encounter your organization? (Describe your ideal client experience from the initial contact throughout their experience with you.)
- What kind of team do you want?
- What are their characteristics and how do they interact with each other, with you, and with your clients?
- What is your facility/workplace like?
- What kind of technology do you have and how are you maximizing it?
- What is your gross and take-home income?
- What is your reputation in your industry or profession, community, state, country, and world? When people think about your organization—or about you personally—what do they think? If someone is seeking your product or service, do they think about you? Do they know how to contact you? Are you easily accessible?

Once you have outlined and imagined this ideal business, ask, "Do I have this now?" If the answer is yes, pat yourself and your team on the back for work well done. However, since we have agreed that there is no such thing as status quo, ask, "How can we do everything we are doing even better?"

The only thing holding us back is the status quo.
—Seth Godin

If you answered, "No, I do not have this ideal business in place," then ask, "What do I need to do to make this happen?" Make the decision to alter things—starting now.

You may find that your existing systems are not functioning in a way that supports your new vision. That's not unusual—or catastrophic! You can implement healthy changes that will move you closer to your ideal. Don't let anything or anyone prevent you from having your ideal business, job, or workplace. You can have this, and you deserve it.

But how can you or anyone who works with you strive toward the ideal if you—or they—are not sure what that means? The more clearly you describe your ideal and the more you move toward it, the better your team will respond. This is vision. This is good leadership.

Shared Vision

A shared vision is a force in people's hearts, a force of impressive power. It may be inspired by an idea, but once it goes further—if it is compelling enough to acquire the support of more than one person—then it is no longer an abstraction. It is palpable. People begin to see it as if it exists. Few if any forces in human affairs are as powerful as shared vision.
—Peter Senge

What a concept! What power! Spend a few moments in your own mind and heart imagining and visualizing how you want your workplace to look, feel, and function! When you visualize your ideal, you have taken the first step toward making that happen. Remember that you become what you think about. You are on your way.

John's Ideal Practice

I'll never forget the day my husband wrote and shared his vision of his ideal dental practice with his team. (I was working in the practice at that time.) John and I had been going through rough financial times during the oil crisis in Oklahoma, and we were really struggling. John practiced in a very small town in rural Oklahoma, and the major industry at that time was oil. However, we did not have the corporate offices or the executives of those oil companies in our area; we had the salt-of-the-earth folks. We had the oil-field workers, farmers, ranchers, teachers, small-business owners, and employees as patients. When the oil crisis hit and the price of oil nose-dived, people moved out of our area in droves.

We published a monthly newsletter, so we could track how many families were leaving by how many returned newsletters we received every month. We had between fifty and seventy-five families moving out of our practice every month. For a small-town business, that was devastating. No one was moving in—and hordes of people were moving out. Our growing, thriving small-town practice slowly and steadily began to go downhill.

I learned a great life lesson during those challenging times. Although our main focus was not on making money—our main focus was taking care of patients and providing a great service—we had to have enough income to keep the doors open, pay our team, purchase supplies, and pay the lab. We also had two kids and a mortgage. We had bills to pay at the office and at home.

If you have never experienced financial stress, let me encourage you never to do so! It's not fun! John and I have experienced many stresses together, but none were more traumatic than major financial stress. We were on the verge of losing everything. We had married in undergraduate school, and I had taught school to put him through dental school. We had started the practice together, established our home, and welcomed our two kids into the world. Things were going great until the bottom fell out.

People still came to him, but they just wanted him to "get them by" until their "ship came in." Stress was over the top. John began to dread going to work.

Expenses piled up. He didn't want to let his team members go. He cared deeply for them and for their families, but paying them became difficult. Bills kept coming in, but the money to pay the bills did not. The more stressed he became at work, the more stressed he became at home. We were on the verge of bankruptcy and on the verge of divorce. When John didn't feel good about himself, he didn't feel good about his practice. He was difficult for his team, and he was unhappy with me. The connectivity of happiness at work and happiness at home was brought to light for us in a personal, painful manner.

Just when we thought we were going to lose it all, John and I decided there had to be a better way. We decided we could throw everything away or we could put ourselves back together and dig ourselves out of the enormous black hole that seemed to be engulfing us.

Miraculously—or divinely—we heard Ed Foreman speak in Dallas. He was like an angel from heaven who appeared just when we were about to fall into that black hole. And he talked about vision and setting goals. They say, "When the student is ready, the teacher appears." Well, we were ready—and he was the perfect teacher.

We thought, *What could it hurt—having this vision stuff, setting these goals? It can't get any worse!* So John wrote out his vision for himself as a dentist, for his patients, for his team, for his practice, for his family, and for his legacy. He called a team meeting, and he read that first "vision statement" to us. It was so beautiful that we all cried—from being so touched by his honesty and his clarity of vision. We went to work to bring that vision into a state of reality.

We worked hard—diligently and with commitment—to improve everything we were doing. We reengineered every system in our practice. We worked on communication skills, marketing, and customer service. We listened to people/patients to find out what they needed and how we could serve them better. We met regularly, as a team, to brainstorm ways to improve. We always paused to celebrate the small victories along the way with a word of appreciation, acknowledgements, notes, and other ways to say, "Hey, good job. Thanks."

In the next year, we increased our business by 50 percent, and the work we did to build our own business became the foundation of the larger business we grew—Jameson Management, Inc.—a corporation focused on helping people in other workplaces find a way to create productive, profitable, stress-controlled businesses that support people in a healthy, fulfilling manner.

It all started with a vision of what could be. Our shared vision motivated us and our team to dig in, work hard, and turn things around. We visualized the ideal and made it happen.

John's practice thrived. His practice became a model practice for people to observe, study, and emulate. We learned so much from those painful times. It was the impetus of that struggle that led us to success.

I now reflect on those times with gratitude. When we learn to face our problems and work diligently toward resolution, there is much learning and growth on the other side. It may have been easier to turn away and run, but I am grateful that we didn't.

What is your vision of your ideal business or position in your company? Write it down and share it with even one person who supports you. It may be inspired by an idea, but once it goes further—if it is compelling enough to acquire the support of more than one person—then it is no longer an abstraction. It is palpable.

The Thinking Pond

I have a special place on our ranch. I call it the "Thinking Pond." It *really is* a pond—about a half a mile away from the house—nestled in the middle of one of the pastures. It's beautiful: surrounded by trees waving in the wind, fish jumping, wildflowers blossoming. Birds, wildlife, and nature quietly and peacefully go about their business of being just what they are intended to be and doing just what they are intended to do. I love the Thinking Pond.

When I have a problem or need to make a major decision, I go to the Thinking Pond to do just that—think. By the time I get to the Thinking Pond, I have often become overwhelmed with emotion regarding an issue. So in the quiet, untouched peace of this special place, Mother Nature wraps me in her arms and supports my efforts.

I sit by the pond, take in all the beauty, and begin my session by counting my blessings. In my mind or right out loud, I count the blessings of my life and express gratitude to God for those blessings. The list of blessings is quite long. Once I have completed my reflection on my blessings, I pose the question or acknowledge my concern. And then—the problem doesn't seem so big, and the decision doesn't seem so difficult. In fact, by the time I have counted my blessings and turn my attention to the decision-making process, the answer is already there. And I am grateful!

What Is Gratitude?

Webster says, "Gratitude is a feeling of thankfulness and appreciation." Studies show that each of us can intentionally develop a state of gratitude. A person's well-being and ultimate happiness can be improved by nurturing this state of gratitude. By acknowledging the things in your life you are grateful for and by expressing your gratitude to others, you can experience increased energy, optimism, and empathy.

Mentally strong people do not waste time feeling sorry for themselves. The research shows that healthy people exchange self-pity for gratitude. They learn from problems and challenges and find strength on the other side.

My personal coach, Alan Cohen, states,

> Gratitude is not a result of things that happen to us; it is an attitude we cultivate by practice. The more we are thankful for, the more we will find to be thankful for. The universe always gives you more of what you are focusing on.

Vision is focusing on the future of your life and your organization. Stop. Be grateful for what you have or for your ability to foresee wonderful things in the future. Believe in possibilities. Express gratitude for the things you have learned—even the difficult lessons. On the other side of the Thinking Pond are insights for a bright future: a healthy work environment.

Creative Opportunities

1. Go to a private place where you can be alone and quiet for a few minutes. Think about your ideal business, ideal job, or ideal life. Take a notebook and pen with you to take notes, if you like.
2. Spend a few minutes thinking about the questions outlined in this chapter. Answer those questions. Make notes, if you choose.
3. Identify things that are going great—and spend moments acknowledging and being grateful for those things. (Even if all you can think of to be grateful for is that you have a job, start there! That's good! Some people don't have a job!)
4. Now identify places for improvement—where you believe the work environment could be healthier for you and for your teammates.
5. Your vision statement will reflect the purpose and the mission you have chosen to pursue.
6. Once you have written your vision for your ideal work environment, move to the next step: setting goals. Here is the heart of strategic planning. The "how do we make that happen?" part of strategic planning.

Be Grateful
By
Cathy Jameson, PhD

Be grateful for this day—it is full of joy.
Awaken yourself to its opportunity.
Be grateful for your health—it is a blessing often taken for granted
Make effort to preserve it.
Be grateful for your many talents.
They often rest under the "bushel basket"—untapped.
Seek to discover and develop your gifts.
Be grateful for your beloved friends—those who are there when you need them.
Be grateful for your family—those who love you unconditionally.
When it's all said and done, they will be beside you.
Be grateful for your work—your chosen career.
Therein lies your opportunity to give back, make a difference, and pursue a purpose.
Be grateful for your challenges—the traumas of life.
These mountains develop your strength, your courage, and your wisdom.
Be grateful for your mind—the director of your being.
Direct your mind with clarity of focus. Your actions will follow proportionately.
Believe it—and it shall be.
Be grateful for God—the Highest of Powers.
Call on Him for direction, guidance, strength, and energy.
Your requests will be heard. Your expressions of gratitude will be valued.
Be grateful for this day.
Be able to look back on it and say, "I'm glad I did …"
Rather than "I wish I had …"
Be grateful.
The joy and opportunity are there.
You must open yourself up in order to see it—and receive it.
Be grateful for your ability to do just that!
Be grateful.

CHAPTER 9

Goal Accomplishment: Part 1

Do. Or do not. There is no try.
—Yoda, *Star Wars*

There are four foundational principles of success. In previous chapters, we have studied the first three: clarity of purpose, mission, and vision. Now we will study the fourth principle: goal setting or goal accomplishment. (I like the intention behind "goal accomplishment" following Yoda's mandate!).

My husband John and I are practitioners of goal setting and have shared that process of goal accomplishment with our business team, our clients, and perhaps most importantly, our children. John and I have worked hard, had trials and tribulations, overcome major and minor obstacles, learned valuable lessons, and rejoiced in the accomplishment of each and every goal, large and small. We celebrate each step taken and the accomplishment of a goal. We are not jealous of each other's successes; rather, we rejoice in each other's accomplishments. We *focus* on what we want in our personal and professional lives through the process of setting goals.

Focus your mind on what you want rather than on what you don't want. The results will reflect your mind-set.

A man is but the product of his thoughts.
What he thinks about he becomes.
—Mahatma Gandhi

The Research Behind the Principle

When transformational leaders set their goals and expectations at a high level, employees tend to set their own sights higher. When the individual members of a team become more productive, the organization becomes more productive as a whole (Jameson, 2010).

Let the vision set forth by the leader infiltrate the organization. Align all processes, decisions, and people with the vision of the ideal organization. Profess the purpose and the mission of the organization so clearly that every act performed inside or outside the organization speaks to the same message (Senge, 2006). All people, all products, all marketing, and all interactions with clients must send the same message. And when the leader sets this tone and consistently represents this vision, other members of the team will do the same.

Webster defined a goal as "the end toward which effort is directed." Goals are the stepping-stones that move you toward fulfillment of your purpose, mission, and vision. Most people have only a vague idea of what they want to achieve in life. Only a handful of people invest the time and the energy necessary to plan for the successful achievement of goals.

Here are the main reasons people do not write their goals:

1. Don't see any reason, don't see the "why"
2. Fear of failure
3. Low feeling of self-worth, lack of confidence, low self-esteem
4. Don't know what their goals are
5. Don't know how

Don't See a Reason or the "Why"

Dr. Gail Matthews of the Dominican University of California performed a study of people who did or did not write goals. Matthews recruited participants from businesses, organizations, and business-networking groups. She drew the following conclusions:

1. People who sent weekly progress reports to a friend accomplished more than those people who did not write goals or who did not have an accountability partner. Results supported accountability.
2. Making a public commitment to a friend regarding written goals also showed significantly more positive results than not making a public commitment. Results supported commitment.
3. People who had written goals and followed a written plan of action accomplished more in measurable entities than people who did not write down their goals. Results supported writing down goals.

The Dominican University research project validated, with empirical evidence, the value of three success tools: accountability, commitment, and writing down one's goals. The results of Dr. Matthews's research showed that people who wrote down their goals and followed a process of goal accomplishment achieved 33 percent more success than those people who did not (Anderson, 2013).

Dr. David McClelland from Harvard University, in studies of motivation, determined that setting goals was a major motivator of people in the workplace. McClelland listed the following benefits of setting goals in today's workplace:

1. motivates employees; they want to be involved in setting and working toward goals
2. offers a time-management strategy

3. supports teamwork
4. offsets procrastination
5. increases productivity of individuals and of the organization itself (McClelland, 1989)

Setting goals is a powerful part of infusing transformational leadership into an organization. Transformational leadership provides a path toward an effective, humanistic approach to leadership by which the goals and aspirations of the people in the workplace can be discovered, acknowledged, and expanded (Bass and Avolio, 1994). People commit to the organization—and to its leaders—rather than posturing compliance (Senge, 2006).

Rather than coming to work for the sole purpose of drawing a paycheck, people who are inspired and motivated by a transformational leader want to be there, contribute, find creative expression in their work, and experience joy and happiness in the workplace. These emotions then transfer to the home and to the families of employees. People in a healthy workplace want to support the creation and fulfillment of goals (Bass and Avolio, 1994).

Fear of Failure and Low Self-Esteem

These are closely related, wouldn't you agree? The inner self-talk of the person who is afraid to write goals because of low self-esteem might go something like this:

> I don't feel great about myself. I'm not sure of myself. I don't want to write down any goals. I don't really believe that I can accomplish this. People will think I'm stupid for writing down that goal. They will wonder, who do you think you are? I'm afraid to make this kind of a commitment to myself and to anyone else. It's easier not to make a commitment,

> and it is a whole lot less risky. I can go along being "average" like the rest of the world, and no one will notice.

The only way to overcome a fear is to face that fear head-on. When people face a fear, address it, and survive, they move toward self-confidence and inner strength. If you, as a leader, write down your goals and follow a process of goal accomplishment, people will model that behavior. If you are apprehensive about writing goals because of your own lack of self-confidence, face your own fears and make an effort to gain confidence: one success, one goal at a time.

Once you begin experiencing your own successes, you will become more committed to the process. People will see what you are accomplishing, and they will see your joy. The joy and enthusiasm that comes from working toward and accomplishing a goal is "catching." You can't buy enthusiasm, but you can catch it!

If you set a goal, but you don't reach it, look carefully at the goal. Do you really want to *do* that or *be* that or *have* that? If so, then look at your plan of action. If the plan didn't get the results you wanted, step back and approach the goal with a different strategy or plan of action. Learn from each plan—the actions that did and did not work. If you approach the goal-accomplishment process with this attitude—one that says you will learn something of value from each victory and from each defeat—you'll be strengthened. Wisdom is a direct result of learning from life's challenges.

Whatever you do, don't quit! Learn from each experience. If you learn to turn negatives into positives, your life will be a constant learning experience. You cannot fail as long as you approach each step positively and with a commitment to learn. However, know that *not* setting goals minimizes your chances of success. The *only* failure is to not set goals at all.

> Only those who dare to fail greatly can ever achieve greatly.
>
> —Robert Kennedy

Don't Know What Their Goals Are

As you begin writing your personal and organizational goals—and encourage your teammates to do the same—set your imagination free. Place every one of your dreams down on paper. Then begin visualizing and analyzing each dream. If you don't think you have any dreams, think again. Reach down deep and pull out any passion you may possess—and write it down. Many people have been programmed to "put away" their dreams and told not to bother with such trivia. I recommend doing just the opposite. Let the dreams surface. Let them out. Imagine.

Until you write down a goal, it is only a dream or a wish. Once you write it down, it becomes better defined. With the power of the mind on your side, you have taken, perhaps, the most critical step in reaching your goals. The subconscious mind does not know the difference between reality and fantasy (James, 2013). Be careful what you put into your mind. Focus on what you do want—and not on what you don't want.

Willpower comes under the realm of the conscious mind, and habit is in the subconscious mind. The subconscious mind is five times stronger than the conscious mind. Make effort to align your subconscious and conscious minds so you have a better chance of reaching your goals. Willpower is the weaker state. Focus continuously on what you want. Visualize the positive results. Over time, the thoughts will become habits and your actions will follow.

Write your goals in the affirmative—as if they have already happened. Day after day, read your goals and plant in your mind's eye the vision of the goal being reached. Hear it, see it, feel it, taste it, and touch it. Use all of your senses to imagine the results. Do not share your goals with anyone who is not supportive. Their negative input will be recorded in your subconscious brain as true. Share your goals with those who you want to support you or who will be part of the process. Share your goals with a trusted accountability partner who will celebrate with you or challenge you (when appropriate). Enthusiastically speak of the end results and benefits of the goal for the organization and for the individual team members.

Writing down the goal serves several purposes:

(a) Writing it down lets you visualize it. It becomes tangible. The mind can begin to focus on reaching the goal.
(b) Written down, you can refer to the goal to evaluate it and make any necessary modifications.
(c) Evaluating your path toward reaching the goal lends a sense of gratification and positive reinforcement for work well done.

Don't Know How

In the next chapter, I outline the steps of goal accomplishment. It's a process: a system. It is one of the most valid, proven, and practical ways of focusing the minds and energies of the people with whom you work—and yourself. Creating a healthy work environment is supported by this enlightened process.

Creative Opportunities

1. Schedule a team meeting where you go over the "why" of goal accomplishment. Share the Dominican University study with the team. Discuss the results of the research.
2. Discuss the reasons people do not write their goals. Uncover ways each of these obstacles can be overcome.
3. Discuss Dr. McClelland's list of benefits of setting goals and identify how each of these could be relevant to your organization. What would these benefits bring to your organization?

4. What does visualization mean to you? Discuss. How do athletes use this principle to prepare for an event? How do musicians use this technique? Why? How could you use this in your organization? What would be the value?

CHAPTER 10

Goal Accomplishment: Part 2 Strategic Planning

Strategic planning will help you fully uncover
your available options, set priorities for them,
and define the methods to achieve them.
—Robert J. McKain

At this phase of goal accomplishment, you are moving from a dream, a wish, a desire, or a "want-to" into the strategic planning stage where—with intention—you can now turn your ideas into tangible results. You have read the theory, the research, and the benefits of setting goals. So now the relevant question is, how do we do this?

Effort and courage are not enough without purpose and direction.
—John F. Kennedy

The How-Tos

Write goals in three separate, yet \related, areas of your life:

- personal and family goals
- business and career goals
- self-improvement goals

These three areas are so interrelated that it is difficult to separate them. How you feel about yourself—your physical, emotional, spiritual, and mental fortitude—definitely affects your work, which in turn affects your family life, and so on. Make supreme effort to keep your life in balance. Decide what *balance* means to you and strive for that worthwhile goal! A healthy work environment is comprised of healthy people who are working to keep balance in their lives.

Aristotle spoke of and wrote about the balance of life. He believed that a healthy balance meant establishing equilibrium and coordinating the four areas of love, work, worship, and play. He believed that at the center of these four areas of life is what all human beings are seeking—and that is happiness.

> Happiness is the meaning and the purpose of
> life, the whole aim of human existence.
> —Aristotle

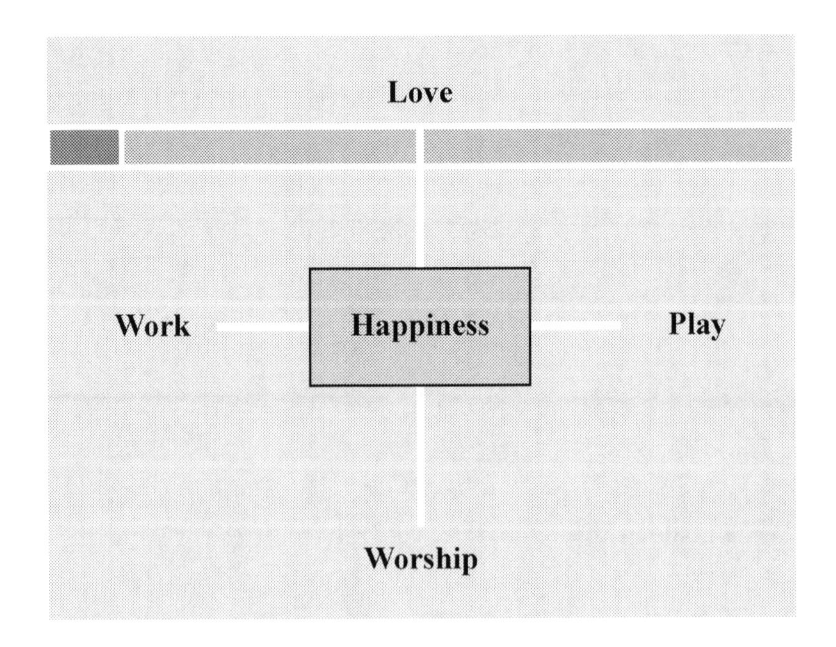

Aristotle

Look again at the three areas where I recommended writing goals: personal and family, business and career, and self-improvement. In each of the three areas, generate thoughts about who and what you want to *be*, what you want to *do*, and what you desire to *have.*

Be, Do, Have

Once you have set your imagination free, once you have reached down deep to pull out your innermost self, write down what it is you want to *be, do,* and *have* in each of those areas. Now put these goals into motion.

The Essential Steps

1. Write the goal. Be specific. Remember that the mind must be able to see the end result of accomplishing this goal. The clearer your written goal—the clearer your expectation of results—the better the outcome. Write the goal in the affirmative as if it has already happened. Visualize what you want to happen. For example, "We have three new offices," "I work out five times per week," or "Our company has accomplished the goal of a 20 percent increase in revenue."
2. Design the plan. Outline the objectives or strategies necessary to accomplish the goal. Determine what action must be taken. What tasks need to be handled? What barriers need to be overcome? What resources need to be accessed? Define all these things in a written plan (the plan of action).
3. Assign responsibilities or determine who needs to do what. Determine the person or persons necessary to carry out the plan and commission them to do so (including yourself).

Assign responsibility and accept that responsibility. Remember to gain the support of an accountability partner. Report to that accountability partner once a week—even with a brief e-mail or text about something you have done to move toward your goal.

4. Time-activate each step of the plan. Assign a time frame for accomplishing each task. This is key to overcoming procrastination. Determine when each aspect of a task needs to be completed. Your time frames may alter when "life happens to you." That's okay. Adjust the plan. But do not quit. Set timelines and deadlines: short-term goals necessary to reach the ultimate goal by the designated time frame.
5. Evaluation: This step is as important—if not more important—than any of the others. How is it going? What have you learned from the proposed plan of action? Do you need to adjust your plan? Continue to do the things that are working and change the things that aren't working.

Your goals may change. That's okay. Keeping the goals written down lets you stay on track and allows you to make changes that are necessary and beneficial.

When I set my goal of receiving a doctoral degree from Walden University, I wrote my goal and a very specific plan of action. The goal did not change, but I did alter the original time frames. The adjustments were necessary and appropriate, but I did not let the alterations discourage me. I adjusted the plan, but I continued with my commitment.

If you are not accomplishing your goal, look back at the goal and ask yourself, "Do I/we really want to do this?" If the answer is yes, then look at your plan of action and make the necessary changes. Keep on doing what is working and change the things that are not working. Adjust. That's fine. Quitting is not.

On the other hand, if you review your goals and find a particular goal that does not resonate with you any longer, it is just fine to put it aside. I've asked myself many times, "I wonder why I wrote that down? I really don't want to do that." If that is the case, then that goal is off the list!

My Father, the Architect

My late father was a brilliant architect whose artistic talents and masterful knowledge of science and engineering became a statement of who he was. He was one of those extraordinary people who left an indelible mark on history and on the lives of those he touched with his work and his love.

I have thought of his profession of architecture and building many times when I teach goal setting. The end result of one of his designs is a beautiful, functional structure serving those for whom the edifice was constructed. When the building is completed, a celebration usually takes place to inaugurate the facility and to share appropriate accolades to the builders, the engineers, and the architect.

However, the process of getting to that point is long and tedious. The process begins many months, perhaps years, before the celebration of the completion. The process begins with an idea (a goal). Then, in a very detailed manner, the architect draws up and writes down specific plans describing to the *n*th degree what must happen before the structure is completed and the goal is accomplished. When the goal is set and the plan is designed, the plan is put into action. Work begins, and specific objectives and strategies are assigned to specific people.

Everyone knows their responsibilities and is held accountable for the accomplishment of their tasks. The team sets a time limit for the accomplishment of each task so the goal of a finished building is met in time to satisfy everyone. Evaluation is an everyday project: How did this fit in with that? How will this portion of the building process prepare us for the next phase? Are we on schedule? Are we heading in the right direction? Do we need to make adjustments in our original plan? When the building is completed—and the goal is accomplished—celebration is in order. And it is good.

I learned great lessons from this man and from his profession: The joy does not come from the end result as much as it comes from the process of doing. The true joy and the ultimate reward is the process of creating: setting the goal, the planning, the building, the development and necessary alterations, and the completion. There is joy in every phase of the journey on the way to the celebration.

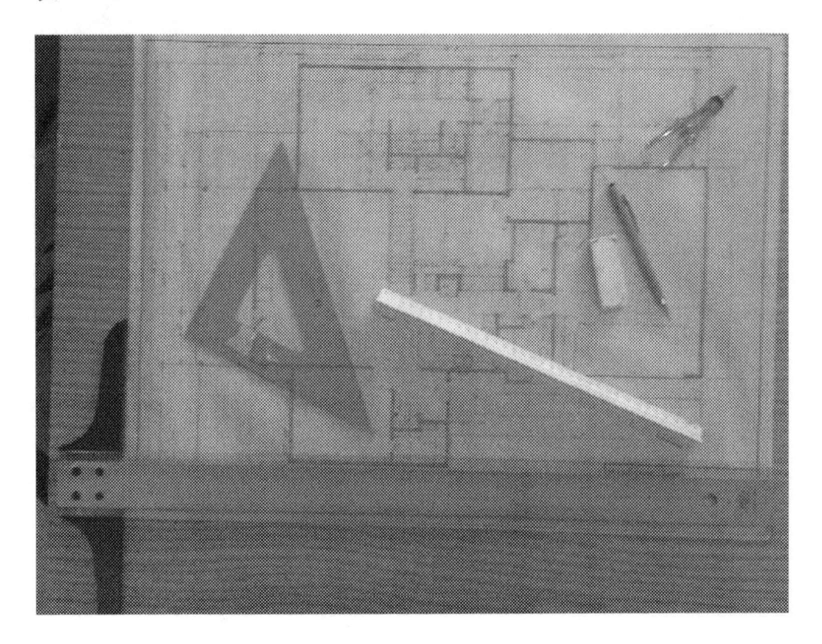

Celebrate the Victories (Even the Small Ones!)

Educators and psychologists have long known that the key to solidifying good behavior is to positively reinforce that good behavior. Each time you take a step forward on your journey to success—when you take a step toward the accomplishment of a goal—pat yourself and your teammates on the back for that forward step. This reinforces your efforts. In working on your self-esteem, this reinforcement gives you a sense of satisfaction that you can do something and do it well. Your efforts have been worthwhile. You get good results for your effort and feel encouraged to continue. You stay motivated.

Celebrate your small victories along the way. You aren't going to go from A to Z overnight. You will need both short-term and long-term goals. But know that each step you take is critical to the whole. And each step takes you closer to the finish line.

Take the time and make the effort to pat one another on the back. If you wait for others to recognize your work, you may wait a very long time. Too often, others are quick to criticize but slow to praise. So when you've accomplished a goal, improved your processes, installed a new system, or put a new service into effect, celebrate the event! Congratulate yourselves, throw your own party, give out gifts, or simply bring in a pizza!

Many team members work behind the scenes. They aren't on the front lines getting immediate feedback from clients. They don't have the visibility and may not get kudos. They keep the ship afloat by making sure bills are paid on time, payroll is completed, checks go out, and information is distributed accurately and in a timely fashion. As the saying goes, no one ever calls to say, "Thanks for getting my check to me on time." It's just expected.

Think of examples of this in your own organization. How can you express appreciation for one another more effectively?

Have your own celebrations when you accomplish certain milestones. Remember to express gratitude for the everyday activities that make it possible for you to perform excellently. Also, remember to be a role model—an example. If you pat others on the back, you set the tone for them to do the same thing.

Ways We Will Celebrate Our Victories

1. ______________________________
2. ______________________________
3. ______________________________

Give immediate reinforcement for work well done and for each step taken forward. This will provide the encouragement to continue on—even if there are difficulties or setbacks. This will also solidify productive behavior and provide encouragement to continue with the next step. Success will breed further success.

Goals and Objectives

Goal:			
Objective	Responsible Person	Time	Evaluation

The form we use in our own business and in our consulting is simple, efficient, and effective.

1. Write the goal.
2. Design the plan.
3. Assign responsibilities for each task.
4. Determine the time to activate each step of the plan.
5. Evaluate your progress.
6. Celebrate the steps along the way, as well as the completion.

Goal Accomplishment

Don't get to the end of your life and look back with regret, wishing you had done something you didn't do or wishing you had spent more time doing something you didn't. When you reach the end of your life, you want to be able to look back and say, "I am so glad I did …" rather than saying, "I wish I had." Plan now to have the life of your dreams. Plan for a healthy work environment and a fulfilled life.

Creative Opportunities

1. Study the art and science of goal setting/goal accomplishment. Become a goal setter yourself. Inspire your entire team to add this productive dimension into their lives and their work.
2. Study the six steps of goal accomplishment. Identify three goals that you would like to accomplish as an organization. Together—or you can break into groups—take the goal sheet included in this chapter and complete the form (as far as you can).
3. If you have broken into groups, get back together and share your written goal with the other groups.
4. Develop accountability partners. Have each person make a commitment to report to his or her accountability partner weekly.
5. Put the agreed plans of action into effect! Just do it!
6. Share in the joy and in the reward of reaching each goal—no matter how large or how small. Brainstorm at least three ways to celebrate your small (or large) victories along the way.

CHAPTER 11

Systems

The success of your business will be in direct
proportion to the success of your systems.
—Cathy Jameson, PhD

Successful Systems: Successful Business

What are systems? Why are they beneficial? How do systems relate to creating a healthy work environment? These are all good and relevant questions. Let's explore each of them.

What Is a System?

> A system is a procedure or process, method, or course of action designed to achieve a specific result. Its component parts and interrelated steps work together for the good of the whole. Creating efficient business systems is the only way to attain results that are consistent, measurable, and ultimately beneficial to customers. They are the building blocks of a company (Carroll, 2015).

Business systems support your purpose, mission, and vision. They are the vehicles for making things happen. Once you have created your purpose, mission, and vision, ask, "Okay, now how do we achieve that? How do we get that done?"

The answer is the goals you set (your strategic plan) and the systems you develop to reach those goals (the system that was outlined for you in the preceding chapters). One of the most important words in Carroll's definition is the word *consistent.* Set up your systems excellently, teach people how to administer them, and measure results. If things are working well, keep on doing those things. If you are not getting the results you want, make necessary changes. Once the systems are working and producing desired results, implement those strategies consistently and with commitment. If the systems are not honored, you are making a choice for things not to go well! Why would you do that?

Efficiency and Effectiveness

Systems refer to the various routines by which the business is managed. These systems may be technical in design, but for the most part, they are administered by people. It is the interaction between the people carrying out their responsibilities that determine effectiveness. Even if you have an unexpected change of staff, your company will not struggle or have a hiccup if the systems are clean and documented—and you have a training program for new employees.

> Organize around business functions not people. Build systems within each business function. Let systems run the business and people run the systems. People come and go, but the systems remain constant.
> —Michael Gerber, *The E-Myth*

Healthy systems that are working well and that are managed by an excellent team are the key to effectiveness and efficiency.

Efficiency relates to getting things done, and effectiveness relates to the energy and focus of the team that engineers those systems.

Without order, the energies of people can be misdirected, resulting in chaos. However, without energy and desire on the part of employees, nothing occurs; rather, inertia sets in. Therefore, energy without focus results in chaos, and focus without energy leads to inertia. Either of these leads to entropy, which *Webster* defines as "lack of order or predictability; gradual decline into disorder." And that's not good!

Entropy can stand in the way of progress, productivity, and organizational success. However, when a business is organized around a functional set of systems—and the leaders and managers make sure the systems support the people who are working those systems—vibrant productivity and energetic employees can result.

- *Effectiveness:*
  Focusing the organization's energy in a particular direction. ***Vision and Direction.***
- *Efficiency:*
  Systems and procedures. The way things are done. Implementation. This starts with the ***vision.***

John Maxwell

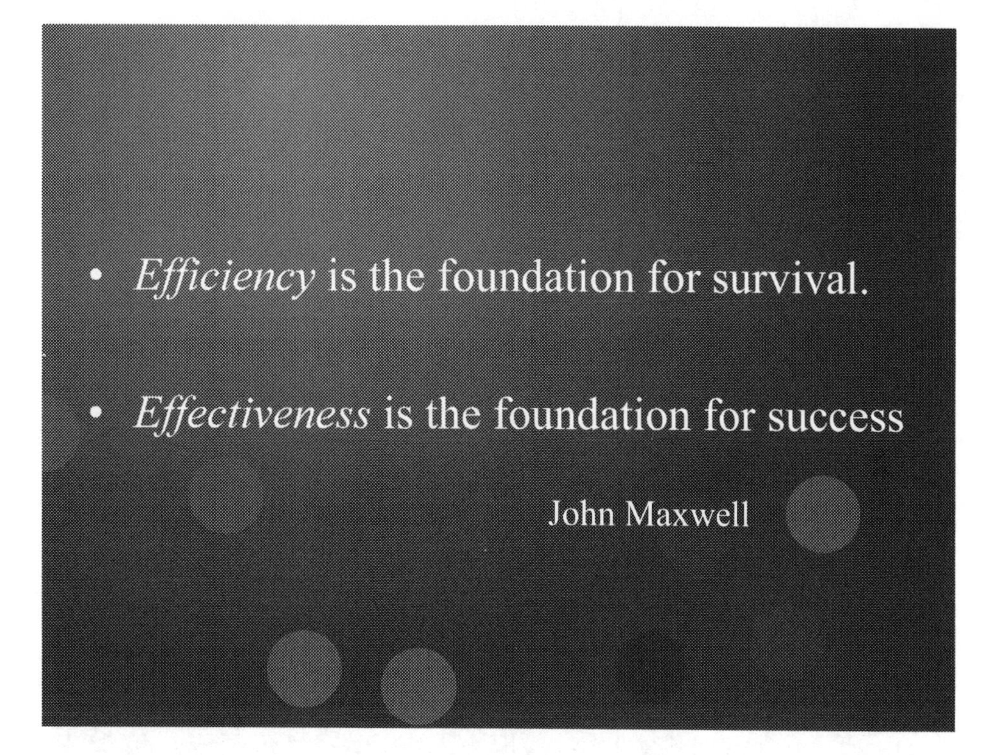

Healthy Systems Equals Stress Control

Some people think that having succinct systems in place will take away from their freedom, their flexibility, and their fun. However, the opposite is true. When you have excellent, well-functioning systems, there are fewer mistakes, better use of time, and maximized talent. People have more room for expression of talent, more time for customer attention, and less stress.

Stress remains a critical issue for organizations, and the negative effects of uncontrolled stress can be debilitating for individuals and organizations. Harris and Kacmar (2006) determined that burnout and dropout are costly to the individual who suffers from stress-related issues and for the company, which may lose a valuable employee. Well-structured and well-administered systems go a long way toward controlling that stress and supporting a stable, productive team.

When the systems are not working well and there is chaos, people feel they are losing control. Their workload seems overwhelming. Redos, mistakes, inefficiencies, and wasted energy are all causes of this feeling. When people get the sense that they will never catch up, the pressure from work continues to build to an exhausting degree. Stress becomes debilitating. Communication often suffers when stress is out of control.

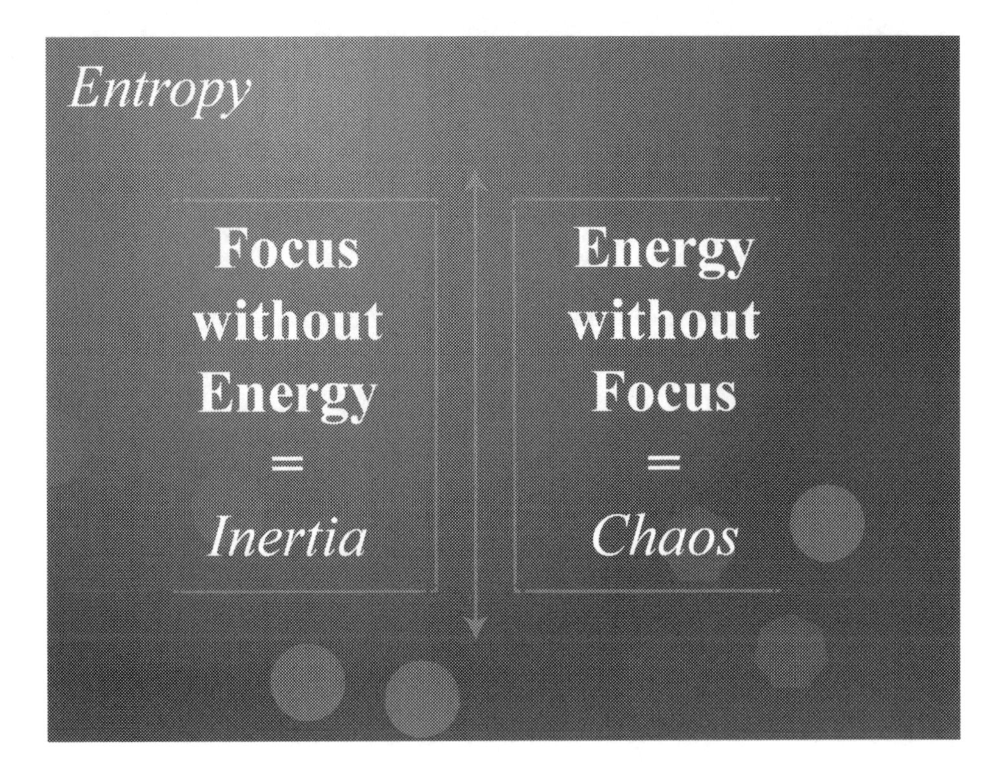

A bad system will beat a good person every time.
—W. Edwards Deming

Inkpen (2005) found that poor or inadequate communication leads to disharmony, feelings of lack of appreciation, confusion of responsibility, and general disorder in the workplace. This leads to increased stress. However, when an organization studies and implements excellent communication skills and implements effective systems, stress diminishes significantly (Jameson, 2000).

1. Set up workable systems in each area of your business.
2. Teach people to administer those systems well.
3. Monitor appropriate data to make sure that predetermined goals that are healthy for the business are being met consistently.
4. If goals are not being met, immediately analyze the system and make adjustments where necessary.

Feedback. A System?

As you are developing and refining your management systems, it is imperative that you provide continuous, helpful feedback to team members who are going to set up or administer those systems. Feedback—or evaluation—is an element of all systems (management and people). An organization is a combination of both.

Positive Feedback

> This very afternoon, while checking my e-mail, I saw that I had been copied on an e-mail from a CEO of an enormous corporation (this was sent to me with permission, of course). He is one of the busiest people I know! The e-mail was a few sentences of inquiry and evaluation about a company project. He thanked his team member for the information that had been provided. He acknowledged that he had taken action on the subject, and he closed by saying, "I appreciate your commitment to our customers and to our team."
>
> The CEO was kept in the loop on a project. He evaluated the situation and took action where necessary. He acknowledged the person and the work that had been done, and he thanked his colleague. He noticed—and said so.
>
> If I received a note like that—I would keep it forever! It may have taken the CEO thirty seconds to type that note, but the effect on that team member will be motivational for eons. It is often the little things that make the biggest difference.

Corrective Feedback

Although positive feedback is vital, so is corrective feedback. Corrective feedback does not mean "blame"—even if the feedback is given when something isn't going too well! Blaming is destructive and is not helpful. Rather, corrective feedback means that if problems in a system are identified, the manager or leader needs to step up to the plate quickly, get to the core of the problem, and move toward resolution. Time passes quickly, and something that isn't working right can cause immeasurable losses. Feedback for successes and feedback when things need alteration are constructive.

1. Communicate with care.
2. Ask permission to meet. Schedule a time.
3. Listen without defensiveness.
4. Avoid negative or blameful language.
5. Be specific: What's happening and the impact of that on you or the company.
6. Act quickly. Don't sit on the problem.
7. Select a private location.
8. Offer support.
9. Decide on specific actions.
10. Evaluate progress in a timely manner.

Feedback gives an organization the opportunity to see when behaviors are supporting progress or are counterproductive to progress. Feedback provides insights into systems that are working and those that are not. Systems are so intertwined that when one system is not working, it can have a negative impact on all other systems and on teamwork. When systems are dysfunctional, this can pit one person or one division against another. In contrast, smooth systems can have a constructive impact all around. People really want the latter. People want to work in an environment where there is compatibility.

When employees respect their supervisors or leaders, they will strive for better performance. In fact, people are often more dedicated to supervisors than they are to organizations (Maslow, 1998). Leaders need to be popular, and they need to create relationships where employees honor, respect, and like them. These employees, consequently, will put in extra effort to get the job done. People do not function well—and productivity cannot advance—in a fear-based environment (Fernando, 2006).

The systems—both managerial and people systems—determine a person's output and dedication. There is a difference between complacent team members and committed team members.

Complacency versus Commitment

Complacency in the workplace leads to a lack of productivity, misused energies, and disappointments. Complacent behavior or complacent people can fall prey to burnout, withdrawal, and boredom. They become lackadaisical. Talent is wasted, and monies spent on training and development may be lost if people are not motivated and, consequently, fall into a pattern of complacency.

Complacent employees may work diligently to do what is expected of them, but they do so with little enthusiasm. They may be compliant, but they often find and focus on what is wrong rather than seeking and reinforcing that which is right. This can lead to dissatisfaction. They become saboteurs who negatively influence their organizations. These people do not address their concerns in a constructive manner with a reconciliatory or problem-resolution goal. Rather, they speak negatively behind the backs of leaders or coworkers and do grave harm to the health and well-being of the company culture. Leaders must stop this negative influence or risk degradation of the organization and loss of productivity.

> Just because some people are fueled by drama doesn't
> mean you have to attend the performance.
> —Cheryl Richardson

However, when people are committed to the vision and to doing their best, they go above and beyond expectations and become viable assets to the organization. Their very presence and performance is valued, which is energizing. These feelings of accomplishment transfer to greater happiness at home and to a sense of personal satisfaction.

> There's a difference between interest and commitment. When you're interested in doing something, you do it only when it's convenient. When your committed to something, you accept no excuses; only results.
> —Kenneth Blanchard

Self-Fulfilling Prophecy

Constructive feedback that supports the development of individuals follows the wisdom of Robert K. Merton who defined the psychological principle of *self-fulfilling prophecy*. Self-fulfilling prophecy means that what is expected of a person or a project will come to pass. If leaders believe that members of their team are outstanding, their performance will become outstanding. When team members receive more attention, better rewards, constructive and validating reinforcement, or encouragement, performance improves. People become what you imagine they can become. Sincerity is obviously a key ingredient here.

Self-Fulfilling Prophecy

Robert K. Merton

"A false definition of the situation evoking a new behavior which makes the originally false conception come true."

Based on the Thomas Theorem (W.I. Thomas)

"If you believe things are real, they are real in their consequences."

Ryan

I taught in the Camelot of schools while John was in dental school. Our administrators and the teaching team all believed in and supported a belief in the self-fulfilling prophecy, and we applied it in our interactions with each other and with our students.

We believed that each student could be successful—and they were. We believed that if any student did poorly, it was not his or her fault; it was our fault. We had somehow not taught them well or had not met their individual needs. Perhaps we had not expressed our belief in their potential to them personally, to their parents, to the administrators, and perhaps to other students, but that was not the case. No one in our school failed.

At the end of my first year of teaching, my principal came to me to share an insight about one of my sixth-grade students. Ryan had done extraordinarily well, and he had proven himself to be a helper to the principal, to me, to other teachers, and to other students. He was a star—and a leader. I never thought he was anything else.

School was out for the summer, and all the kids were gone. My principal told me that Ryan had been transferred to our school because he had been such a disciplinary problem and a "failure" at his previous school that they would not let him attend there anymore. He was labeled a "delinquent." My principal had not given me (or any of our teachers) records of the students coming to us (it was our first year as a new school). We had no preconceived notions about any of the students. We believed that all the students could and would be successful, cooperative, and good citizens. That was our belief, and that self-fulfilling prophecy was, indeed, fulfilled.

We had not judged Ryan as a delinquent. We treated him as a respected, loved, honored young man and believed he could and would be a successful student—and he became just that.

The principle of self-fulfilling prophecy is applicable to home, work, school, and personal relationships. People can become more than they imagine possible when another person believes in them. If you work with people from that perspective—and belief—you'll have a company full of Ryans.

The same is true of projects—and of companies! Big-thinking projects become possible when the team believes success will result. Starting with the leader. Steve Jobs said, "I want to put a dent in the universe." He was a big thinker.

The law of attraction says, "You become what you think about most, and you also attract what you think about most."

Tell your team members what they *can* do—and they will respond. If you tell people what they *can't do,* they will respond in kind!

Whether you think you can, or you think you can't—you're right.
—Henry Ford

Technical systems alone are not the answer to success. The answer is systems managed by enthusiastic employees or knowledge workers who feel they are contributing to the success of the whole. As Drucker (1999) pointed out, "One does not manage people. The task is to lead people. And the goal is to make productive the specific strengths and knowledge of each individual." Business-management systems and people systems are essential for creating a healthy work environment.

Creative Opportunities

1. Read the opening three questions again: What are systems? Why are they beneficial? How do systems relate to *Creating a Healthy Work Environment*? Now that you have read this chapter, discuss each. Give your opinion.
2. Business systems and people systems were discussed and encouraged. What are the differences? What are the similarities?
3. Why are both essential? How are they related?
4. Write down the major systems of your own company. Identify the ones that are working well. Identify the ones that could use some improvement. What could you do to take the first step toward improvement? Decide how you will do just that.
5. What is a self-fulfilling prophecy? Give an example. Identify one way you can put the self-fulfilling prophecy to work in your own life—personally or professionally. What is one action the company can take to implement this truism of human behavior? How would that be beneficial?

CHAPTER 12

Communication

Speak with honesty. Think with sincerity. Act with integrity.
—*A Course in Miracles*

Clear, constructive communication is a valuable asset for a healthy team and a healthy work environment. The systems of your organization, including systems of communication, need to be established, administered, and evaluated. Interoffice or intercompany communication that informs and supports all systems is imperative (Senge, 2006). Resources need to be made available to provide this support. People cannot be expected to remain motivated or to achieve success if they don't have the resources they need, such as money, technology, proper training and education, support, and *continuous communication* (Herzberg, 1966).

Teamwork is the ability to work together toward a common vision. The ability to direct individual accomplishment toward organizational objectives. It is the fuel that allows common people to attain uncommon results.
—Andrew Carnegie

Bennis and Nanus (1997) identified the following specific stages or strategies of teamwork:

- focusing attention on clarity of vision
- developing trust through positioning
- encouraging a sense of self-confidence based on a principle of discovery without failure
- establishing meaning through constant communication

I will address all four of these elements in this book, but for now, let's look at the fourth characteristic—communication, a critical factor in any business.

Communication: The Bottom Line to Success

In my book, *Great Communication Equals Great Production,* I hypothesized that when the leader or the entire team study and implement improved communication skills, productivity increases individually and collectively (Jameson, 2004). In addition, when an organization studies transformational leadership, which includes the study of communication skills, productivity of the organization increases (Jameson, 2010). Transformational leadership and great communication go hand in hand to create great production.

For me, the opportunity to improve communication is a lifelong study. Would you agree? I don't think I will ever be as good at communication as I want or need to be. How about you?

Communication has many aspects or elements. Approximately 60 percent of any message—whether you are sending or receiving it—is body language; 30 percent is tone of voice; and 10 percent is the words you speak. Of course, the words you speak are critical. A misspoken word can enhance a relationship or destroy it. A harsh, inappropriate word can remain a source of pain in a person forever. Be careful. Choose your words carefully. Pause before you speak. However, it is the entire message that counts: the words, the body language, and the tone of voice. All are worthy of attention.

Becoming an excellent communicator is worth the effort if you agree that relationships are vital to a fulfilled life. The benefits include:

- improving personal relationships at work and at home
- developing a more cohesive team or family
- reducing burnout and dropout for yourself and your team members
- reducing stress for everyone in your organization and home
- increasing productivity by a minimum of 10 percent
- having more clients make a decision to buy your product or service or to work with you
- having clients agree to their financial responsibility, reducing disagreements regarding money
- developing "engaged" employees and "engaged" clients
- preserving relationships and cultivating "retention"

What Is Communication?

Communication is an exchange of information and feelings. A message is sent, and a message is received. Send messages clearly and succinctly. Deliver your message carefully. Make sure it is understood clearly and accurately. "Just because someone says they understand, doesn't mean they do" (Jameson, 2010).

When you receive a message from someone, listen with focus, attentiveness, and empathy. Your interactions with other people—teammates and clients—remains at the core of a healthy organization. The world is digital, but human interaction will, hopefully, always involve one-on-one, face-to-face exchanges and connectedness, supported by great communication.

> I fear the day that technology will surpass our human interaction. The world will have a generation of idiots.
>
> —Albert Einstein

Communication: A Four-Part Series

There are four things we do with language: read, write, speak, and listen. Let's look at these more closely.

Reading and Writing

In today's digital world, we read and write constantly on our mobile devices: smartphones, computers, tablets, and other mobile devices. In your business, you have multiple written pieces of informational or marketing data that describe and promote your business. Your advertising—no matter the medium—is written. You exchange information through memos, e-mails, texting, e-zines, blogs, e-newsletters, and social media. You continuously interact with team members or clients through the written word.

Many miscommunications can be eliminated if the written information (computerized or handwritten) is comprehensive and accurate. Evaluate your written communications and ask, "Is internal information being shared in a succinct, thorough manner? Is it clear enough that people are not constantly asking us to explain, clarify, or fill in the blanks?" A digital message is meant to provide data.

- Our team meeting time has changed from 2:00 p.m. to 3:00 p.m. tomorrow, June 23.
- I will meet you at the Greenhouse Restaurant at 7:00 p.m. Two guests will be joining us.
- Thank you for the time you spent with me yesterday. Our brainstorming session was innovative and thought provoking. I'd like to review your third suggestion again. Is there a time that is good for you this week? Let me know. Looking forward to working further on this project.

Speaking

Nido Qubein (1997) said, "To achieve precision and effectiveness in communicating, you should understand the basic process of communication. It has four requirements:

- A message must be conveyed.
- The message must be received.
- There must be a response.
- Each message must be understood."

When you speak, get your message across clearly. Do your best to eliminate misunderstanding or inaccuracy. When something is causing a problem, express that concern without hurting the other person or turning a misspoken word into a conflict.

The goals of good speaking are the following:

- to help people want to listen to what you have to say
- to deliver the message in the best possible way
- to check to see if you were heard (or interpreted) correctly

In order to do that, you must do the following:

- get to the point
- be specific
- be positive
- present your recommendations to the other person's motivators
- establish and protect a relationship of trust with your colleagues and clients (Jameson, 2004).

When you are addressing a person or addressing a challenging issue, the goal is to maintain the relationship and solve the problem. You can say something one way and get a positive response or say something in another way and get a negative response. How you say anything makes a powerful difference.

If you have a problem or are upset with someone, do not address it in an e-mail! If 60 percent of a message is body language and 30 percent is tone of voice, that means 90 percent of the perception of a message—whether you are sending or receiving it—is everything but the words. A message can be easily misinterpreted. Digital communication is not meant for solving problems.

Texting is a brilliant way to miscommunicate how you feel and misinterpret what other people mean.

Listening

"Listen before you speak. Understand. Diagnose. Listen with your ears—and your eyes and your heart. Find out what the most important behaviors are to the people you're working with. Don't assume you know what matters most to others. Don't presume you have all the answers—or all the questions" (Covey and Merrill, 2006).

Listening to the whole person is as important as hearing the words. Listening is essential if you are trying to determine the emotional hot button or major motivator of a client or patient. If you have a situation that is difficult, listening is the single best way to reduce intensity of emotion. When emotion is too intense, it can cloud the messages being sent or received.

Listening may be the greatest gift we can give one another, but it's not easy. Many things get in the way of good listening: time, busy schedules, interruptions, being unfocused, too much going on at one time, not wanting to listen, being in a hurry to give a solution rather than listening, and egotistically thinking you already know the answer so you don't have to listen.

Interestingly, in spite of the value of listening, most people have never had a course on listening. We all study reading, writing, and speaking, but how many people have ever had a course on listening? We just assume that since we have our "ears on," we are listening. You may be *hearing*, but that is not *listening*.

In a study of motivation, called the Hawthorne effect, Dr. Elton Mayo said, "One friend, one person who is truly understanding and who takes the trouble to listen to us as we consider our problem, can change our whole outlook on the world."

Did I get that right?

How many times do we hear the words that another person speaks but totally misinterpret the meaning? Get out of your own way and give your total focus to the person speaking. Then, once someone has finished talking, paraphrase what you "think" he or she said and feed it back to the person. Don't just repeat the words verbatim. That is offensive and ineffective.

Instead, empathize. Listen for the content of the message and the feeling behind it to see if you are hearing the person accurately. The operative word is *accurate*. Don't assume you heard things correctly. A minister friend of mine says, "Assumption is the lowest form of human communication."

The time and effort put into listening with care and accuracy will save you time in the long run and will go a long way toward building a relationship of trust and confidence. This includes

- showing respect
- establishing clear meaning
- capturing the intention of a statement or message
- furthering the relationship
- reducing mistakes

Eight Steps to Effective Listening

1. Reduce as many distractions and interruptions as possible.
2. Focus your mind on the speaker. Clear away as many internal distractions as possible.
3. Take note of key issues so you stay focused and can return to the points when appropriate.
4. Respond to the speaker's total message. Do not pay attention to the words only. Pay attention to the body language, tone of voice, and emotion.
5. Listen without judgment.
6. Do not be thinking about what you are going to say or how you are going to respond. You will be unable to accurately listen.
7. Keep an open mind when you are listening to another.
8. If you catch yourself not listening, refocus and change your body position to make it more conducive to listening.

A Lifelong Study

Truly, the study of communication is a lifelong—and worthwhile—study. If people in the workplace are going to get along, support one another, be productive, and promote the growth of the business, excellent communication will be at the heart of every interaction.

The game of life is a game of boomerangs. All our thoughts, deeds, and words return to us sooner or later with astounding accuracy.
—Florence Scovel Shinn

Great communication equals great results, great relationships, and great production. Great communication is part of creating a healthy work environment.

Creative Opportunities

1. Have team members define what communication means to them.
2. As a team, discuss the importance of communicating with each other and with clients.
3. Discuss the four types of communication (reading, writing, speaking, and listening). Discuss what is going well so you can continue to do those things. Discuss areas where improvement could be beneficial and what you will do to support that improvement.
4. Read the eight steps to effective listening and discuss how and why these are valuable to you as colleagues and how these principles of good listening could support your interactions with clients.
5. What does "great communication equals great production" mean to you? Translate that as a tangible asset to your organization.

CHAPTER 13

Trust

When wealth is lost, nothing is lost.
When health is lost, something is lost.
When character is lost, all is lost.
—Billy Graham

Trust

In a healthy work environment, people want to trust and be trusted. Trust is "a firm belief in the reliability, truth, ability, or strength of someone or something."

In a healthy work environment, people can "count on others to do the things they say they will do." Employers want to trust that their employees are honorable, trustworthy, and accountable. And the same is true in reverse. Trust says, "I am who I am—no matter where I am or who I am with." Your deeds and actions match your words. What you do and say are the same, and they match up.

What are the core values of your business? Do people in your organization know? If I asked them, could they tell me? Are your core values (the ones you wrote for your mission statement) reflected each day in every interaction with colleagues or customers? If not, which customer is going to get the short end of the stick? And why him or her?

Lack of Trust? Stressful?

There may be no greater cause of stress in the workplace than lack of trust! Unbelievable stress develops if the employer doesn't know the following:

- people are doing what they are supposed to do
- people are handling customers in the best possible manner
- monies are being properly and ethically managed
- correct information and data are being entered, transferred, or submitted

Oftentimes, the employer is in a separate location or in a separate part of the office when business is transpiring. They can't do everything themselves or worry about things being done properly. They don't want to micromanage, and employees don't want to be micromanaged.

That's where trust comes in. I was working with a company in the eastern part of the United States. The owner/president was so stressed from his work that he wanted to run away and hide. He had lost his love for his profession, and he didn't even want to come to the office. His stress did not come from his customers; he enjoyed his interactions with them.

However, mismanagement and unreliable members of his "staff" (I cannot call them a team) were causing him to be sick from overwhelming stress. He never knew what was happening with clients—on the phone or in person—and he didn't know if monies and accounts were being managed properly. He didn't know if people were fulfilling their roles, and he didn't trust anyone. He was staying late to double-check everything and taking work home at night to double-check it. He was burning himself out.

He didn't trust his employees, and they did not trust him (a self-fulfilling prophecy). The entire business was in a vicious cycle of unhealthy interactions that helped no one. Ultimately, there was a revolving door of employees.

The owner believed the problem was simply that "there are no good people out there," but I begged to differ. There *are* good people out there. But the culture of a healthy business has to be built on trust, and trust needs to be modeled and supported. Mutual trust translates to effort, quality performance, and good communication.

The story has a happy ending.

- We defined his purpose, mission, and vision.
- We helped the team set goals for themselves and the company.
- We established excellent systems throughout the company and spent appropriate time training people how to administer each system.
- We established monitors to determine if the systems were working and if people were performing well, thereby reaching our goals.

Throughout the process, we studied, practiced, and refined all communication skills. Position responsibilities were carefully aligned with people's skills, talents, and interests. The owner was able to focus on the things that only he could do. He monitored the results and refined things where needed. He and I studied leadership skills, and we brought the team into those study sessions at appropriate times.

The business grew substantially. He was happy, and so was the team. It was truly a happy movement in the right direction. The trust that had been lost by the team was recuperated. That was not easy. Trust is hard to gain, easy to lose, and even harder to regain, but over time, the trust was reestablished. Without trust, the company could never have moved forward. The end result would have been a lot of burned-out people who were ready to leave, including the owner!

Is trust imperative to a healthy work environment?

I decided to survey the team members of The Jameson Group, our own company, to ask them that question.

Our team members travel throughout the United States and the world, working with businesses and teams. We provide management, marketing, clinical and technological training and education, as well as teamwork and leadership coaching.

I wanted to hear from our own team members to get their perceptions of this principle of trust in the workplace. The mission of our company is to increase productivity, increase profitability, and control stress. We coach businesses in how to integrate proven systems of business management. However, without a foundation of excellent teamwork, leadership, and communication, we cannot help businesses reach their ultimate potential. At the heart of this development is trust.

I gathered several of my team members and asked, "What does trust mean to you as a member of The Jameson Group—and what does trust mean in the businesses you coach?

Nancy Dukes, Registered Dental Hygienist, Certified Business Manager, and Senior Consultant

- Being able to trust that your employer is going to support you even in difficult times.
- Knowing that you have a safe environment where you can ask for help if you need further training.
- Having systems of communication in place so that communication can be regular, open, and honest.
- Having an environment of appreciation and praise.
- Having an environment where individuals are encouraged to grow, develop, and strive to reach their full potential.
- Knowing that there is no room for negativity.
- Teamwork is the culture.

Becky Speer, Registered Dental Hygienist and Senior Consultant

- Having a firm belief in the character and integrity of the people and the organization.
- Having an understanding and clarity about the vision of the organization and knowing that the vision is consistently honored in all things.
- Building relationships with teams and patients is an integral part of creating trust. It takes time to build trust—but only a second to break it.

Beverly Hill, Senior Business Consultant and Certified Business Manager

- Trust is knowing that when I am given a responsibility or task, my coworkers and employers will know, without a doubt, that I will complete a task or responsibility with all my energy and focus.
- It also means that my employer has empowered me and knows that I can be relied on to carry out whatever responsibility is given to me.
- There is no need for policing or riding herd over me to be assured that I am doing what is expected.
- Trust also means that, as an employee, I am confident my employer is making decisions based on what is best for the company and for the team.

Amy Logan-Parrish, Senior Vice President of Development

- Not micromanaging tasks or projects. Once a request has been made, trust that the task will get done and get done in a timely manner, rather than having to ask or be asked about it over and over.
- Trust is demonstrated when a task is delegated and completed without hovering or micromanaging. This can be challenging for the trainer sometimes, as giving up that control can be hard. Yet once you do, you have time to do the other things on your plate that need attention, and you are developing another trusted leader in your organization.

Andrea Greer, Registered Dental Hygienist, Certified Computer Trainer, and Senior Consultant

- My teammates can believe without fail that I will be approachable and not "blow a gasket" if someone brings a concern to me about our interaction.
- I won't give a person the silent treatment or gossip to someone else if a teammate is being honest and open with me about something I may have said or done to upset them.
- When I say I am trusting, I am assuring my teammates that I am counting on them to come to me directly when an issue arises.
- I need to trust that my teammates won't gossip to others or pretend they aren't upset. I am trusting that they will keep the lines of communication open.

Dr. Mark Hyman, Private Practitioner in Greensboro, NC, International Speaker, Client of The Jameson Group

Trust:

- When you trust your team, you thrive.
- Without trust, you practice alone.
- Trust means love.
- Trust means abundance.
- Trust means success.

Are trust and integrity related?

Yes. But where is integrity in today's world? We see breaches of trust and confidence in large and small businesses, compromising values to make more money, cutting quality to reduce costs and increase profits (even though the client/customer/patient suffers), and falsifying information so executives can make huge bonuses to the detriment of clients who placed trust (and their hard-earned money) into their hands. Where is the integrity that refuses to harm innocent people so that those "in charge" can make more money?

Trust and integrity are interrelated. Without integrity, trust is absent. When integrity is present, the values that make up the very soul of a person are honored instead of destroyed.

I was raised by wonderful parents. In our home, there was no compromise of integrity. We learned that if we were not honest with others, we could never honor ourselves. In the end, it is our integrity that will live on and leave behind a legacy of goodness. My father lived the integrity he learned from his parents, which was supported in his service to our country in the United States Marine Corps.

Dad joined the Marines on the day he turned eighteen, and he served during World War II. He incorporated the ethics and integrity of his service as a marine into every fiber of his life: his family, community, and business.

The values of the Marine Corps are based on three values: honor, courage, and commitment.

Honor requires each Marine to exemplify the ultimate standard in ethical and moral conduct. Honor is many things, and honor requires many things. A marine must never lie, cheat, or steal, but that is not enough. Much more is required. Each marine must cling to an uncompromising code of *personal integrity*, being accountable for personal actions and holding others accountable for theirs.

And above all, honor mandates a marine never sully the reputation of the United States Marine Corps.

Courage is honor in action—and more. Courage is moral strength, the will to heed the inner voice of conscience, and the will to do what is right regardless of the conduct of others. It is mental discipline, an adherence to a higher standard. Courage means willingness to take a stand for what is right in spite of adverse consequences. Throughout the history of the United States Marine Corps, this courage has sustained marines during the chaos, perils, and hardships of combat. And each day, it enables each marine to look in the mirror—and smile.

Commitment means total dedication to United States Marine Corps and the United States. Gung-ho marine teamwork. All for one, one for all. By whatever name or cliché, commitment is a combination of selfless determination and relentless dedication to excellence. Marines never give up, never give in, and never willingly accept second best. Excellence is always the goal. When their active-duty days are over, marines remain reserve marines, retired marines, or marine veterans. There is no such thing as an ex-marine or former marine. Once a marine, always a marine. Commitment never dies (Sturkey, 2009).

As you read this credo of the US Marine Corps, can you see how these values transfer or translate to your own life—personally and professionally—and to your business?

In a workplace based on integrity, the owners and employees have nothing to hide. There is openness and disclosure. The values that are the backbone of the company are evident to all who work there and to all clients. The integrity of the company is not about "what we do" but rather "who we are," and who we are determines what we do (Covey, 1989). Conduct mirrors beliefs and values. Trust is created in an environment that stands on this truth.

The following diagram lists characteristics of a person/company with integrity: characteristics that build and sustain trust.

Integrity

- Singlemindedness
- Nothing to hide/nothing to fear
- A system of values against which all of life is judged
- Not "what we do" but rather "who we are" and "who we are" determines "what we do."
- Our beliefs are mirrored by our conduct.

Integrity

- Has high influence value
- Facilitates high standards
- Results in a solid reputation, not just image
- Living it before leading others
- A hard won achievement
- Builds trust

—John Maxwell

People want to be trusted. They want the respect that is at the core of a trusting environment. People cannot function well in a place where they are humiliated in front of others or where they fear that if they make a mistake, they will be fired, ridiculed, or "ripped to shreds." Certainly, if a person makes a mistake or is doing things incorrectly, that behavior or performance needs further attention, expanded instruction, and correction of whatever is not being done properly. But a fear-based management style is the least effective of any management method. If people live in fear, they will never stretch, grow, or be creative.

If my people understand me, I'll get their attention.
If my people trust me, I'll get their action.
—Cavett Roberts

Be on the side of your colleagues; they are your teammates. Have each other's backs. Be a protagonist rather than an antagonist. Happiness in the workplace is possible. When you build people up by creating an environment of trust, you take a major step in creating a healthy work environment.

Creative Opportunities

1. Discuss the definition of trust. What is trust? What does it mean to you personally and to your business?
2. What do you do to nurture and support trust between and among the people in the organization? Be specific. Give examples.
3. What are the benefits of these things to employees? To employers? To the business itself?
4. Identify an area—or a specific issue—where there is a lack of trust. What is happening? What is not happening? Be honest with each other and work to develop a clear plan of action to alter that state. Commit to making alterations that will build greater trust.
5. Are there differences between integrity and trust? What are those differences? Are these two characteristics—trust and integrity—related? How? Give an example.

CHAPTER 14

Appreciation

As we express our gratitude, we must never forget that the
highest appreciation is not to utter words, but to live by them.
—John F. Kennedy

A healthy work environment advocates the psychological, physical, and financial health of employees. Without healthy employees, the organization cannot maximize its potential. The nurturing of employees translates into the nurturing of the organization itself (Maslow, 2000). Of course, if the company isn't productive and profitable, it cannot stay in business. If that happens, no one wins because no one has a job! It takes everyone working together—cohesively—to make things work and work well.

The more you are grateful for what you have,
the more you will have to be grateful for.
—Zig Ziglar

A healthy work environment is best when built on excellent teamwork, support, friendships, unified spirit, pride, commitment, and teammates (Drucker, 1999). When knowledge workers feel their contributions are valuable and significant, they will deliver on work requirements in a more compassionate and energetic manner.

An effective leader encourages people, nurtures talent, and creates a supportive culture that develops committed employees. People want and need to feel proud of their own work and of their company (Joseph and Linley, 2006).

On the Other Hand

When the mode of operation is to embarrass and reprimand people when they make mistakes, this diminishes self-esteem and people cannot thrive (Joseph and Linley, 2006). Instruction, education, and positive reinforcement move people toward constructive effort and accurate results. If the work environment does not support this and is managed with negativity, authoritarianism, and hostility, people will leave. Knowledge workers today want to have fun at work, and if it is not enjoyable—or if they dread going to work—they will not stay (Jameson, 2010)

Leaders and managers often focus on the profitability of the organization and on numerical, measurable factors. However, when leaders understand and appreciate behavioral issues and how they affect attitude and performance, energy and productivity are generated through satisfied employees (Hartline and Ferrell, 1996). Now, *that* enhances the bottom line!

This is reciprocal as well. Employers, bosses, and executives work hard. They have unbelievable stress and responsibilities. They need to be recognized and reinforced. Just because there is a "Boss's Day" does not mean it is the only time of year that a boss needs to hear employees say, "Thank you."

Individualized Recognition

Recognition needs to be individualized specifically for the person and for his or her accomplishments. When recognition is personalized, the incentive is more meaningful and effective (Strumpfer, 2005).

What does it mean to individualize the type of recognition given? Different people—by their natures and personality types—may want and need to be recognized in different ways. Some people would be embarrassed by public recognition, whereas others are quite proud to receive public acknowledgment. Some people would rather have a note than a luncheon in a restaurant. Recognition can be given before thousands, in small meetings, or at intimate luncheons with the team. Do your best to find out what motivates the different people in your division or company—and individualize your appreciation.

When I studied education at the bachelor's and master's level, I learned about individualized instruction. Simply said, if everyone is taught or managed in the same manner, someone will lose out. Why? Everyone is different, and everyone learns and is motivated in different ways. It is up to the instructors, teachers, and leaders to determine those "uniquenesses" and individualize them according to the various people on the team. Tough to do? Not really. Just keep your eyes and ears open. Listen to people's words and pay attention to their behaviors. Be more interested in others than you are in yourself—and you will gain great insight.

The greatest gift you can give another is
the purity of your attention.
—Richard Moss

Cohen (2006) found that many managers and leaders *believe* their employees are best rewarded with money. However, this is not often the case. Recognition for accomplishments and expressions of appreciation are more effective and have longer-lasting effects than monetary or physical rewards. Cohen found that when employees received rewards that were not monetary, they sensed greater recognition for their accomplishments. Recognition from their employers led them to feel appreciated for their work and for the time invested in tasks. Immediate reinforcement for work well done is intrinsically motivational. It feels good in the gut. These kinds of rewards are only effective if they are individualized for particular employees. In addition, the employee or teammate who is being rewarded must truly be worthy of the reward or recognition.

Knowledge workers want to feel valuable and be seen as significant to the whole. They want to work in safe environments without fear of anger, hostility, or fighting. They want to have open channels of communication when problems arise. The worker of today wants to have fun at work and be a part of an organization that is touching others in positive ways. They want to know that they can leave a legacy and make the world a better place because of their own efforts and their participation in the organization (Maslow, 2000).

In an environment committed to enlightenment, appreciation is expressed sincerely and regularly. People are involved because they want to be. They find this stimulating and challenging. People can maximize their talents. They can stretch and explore possibilities. They do not get bored and yearn to move to another location. A different kind of leadership is required for these principles of enlightened management to take place. Leaders must transform to an effective enlightened leadership modality: transformational leadership.

In his management classic, *The GMP: The Greatest Management Principle in the World,* Dr. Michael LeBoeuf says, "That which is rewarded is repeated." If you notice something good, say something.

If someone is making progress toward a goal, thank the person. Encourage him or her. Reinforce that progress. That's the best reward of all.

Lawrence Lindahl performed a benchmark study decades ago. His research project has been repeated many times, and the results have remained steadfast. This is the mark of a substantial and measurable research project. Lindahl wanted to know what *employees* found motivational. He wanted to know what *employers* thought would be motivational for the people who worked for and with them. The differences are astounding.

What employers think motivates employees:

1. Good wages
2. Job security
3. Promotion/growth opportunities
4. Good working conditions
5. Interesting work
6. Personal loyalty to workers
7. Tactful discipline
8. Full appreciation for work well done
9. Sympathetic help with personal problems
10. Feeling "in" on things

What employees think motivates employees:

1. Full appreciation for work well done
2. Feeling "in" on things
3. Sympathetic help on personal problems
4. Job security
5. Good wages
6. Interesting work
7. Promotion/growth opportunities
8. Personal loyalty to workers
9. Good working conditions
10. Tactful discipline

Appreciation

Look at the differences between what employees said was important to them and what employers thought! Employers thought money was most important—and, of course, it is important. However, employees rated money fifth. They do have to put food on the table, a roof over their heads, and shoes on their kids' feet (and those tennis shoes aren't cheap!). Employers thought appreciation was eighth, but employees said it was first! In other words, employees will leave an organization because they do not feel appreciated much more quickly than they will leave an organization to make more money down the street. If someone leaves your organization to make more money down the street, more than likely, there was something else wrong in the situation. Something else was missing (unless the money difference was extremely measurable). Money is important—employees ranked it fifth—but appreciation was ranked first. Both are important. A combination of compliments and cash goes a long way!

In *The One Minute Manager Builds High Performing Teams,* Dr. Ken Blanchard said, "We find it so easy to catch each other doing something wrong. Why don't we catch each other doing something right?" I agree. However, the ability and willingness to express appreciation is not always the norm. In fact, there are those who believe that if you don't say something to coworkers or employees, they will automatically think they are doing things right. Well, that's not actually true. People do not always know if they are doing things well or if their performance is pleasing you. I have had some employers actually say, "Well, if I don't tell her she's doing something wrong, she must know she is doing things right." Psychologically, no reinforcement is perceived as negative reinforcement. Not saying anything at all is not effective—and can be counterproductive.

Some leaders and managers tell me they simply don't know how to give compliments or provide positive reinforcement. Maybe they have never received any positive reinforcement themselves and have nothing to model. However, this can be a learned skill. It's a good skill to learn and use!

People can express appreciation in many ways. It does not have to be money. It *can* be money, but it does not have to be money. In fact, other ways of showing appreciation are more beneficial and rewarding. Let's look at a few of the thousands of ways to express appreciation. You will have your own ways. That's great. Get in the *habit* of expressing appreciation.

1. Say so! Dale Carnegie says a compliment is "a statement of appreciation backed up by evidence." In other words, tell the person that you appreciate them and what you liked or valued: "Virginia, I appreciate your professional demeanor and gracious, patient way of answering all my questions." "John, when you complete those reports so excellently and present them to me on time, it helps us move the project along more quickly. Thanks."
2. A written note of appreciation, a line or two indicating gratitude or acknowledging someone's effort, goes a long way to encouraging that person. No matter how strong a person's self-esteem, everyone benefits from being recognized, being thanked, and being appreciated.

3. Send an e-mail or a text of gratitude.
4. Give someone a gift certificate, a lunch, or a present when appropriate. When you express appreciation, be specific. Tell the person you are grateful or pleased and be specific about what stimulated your gratitude: “Carrie, I appreciate your careful effort to make sure this blog is done correctly and that people are able to receive the blog in a clear and timely fashion. Great job. Thanks.”

Express sincere appreciation for the specific thing for which you are grateful. The operative word here is *sincere*. This kind of compliment is not manipulative; it is giving an honest expression of appreciation to someone who deserves it. Start with one compliment. Then another. Pretty soon, what may have seemed weird to you will become natural. The entire process of “statements and actions that express appreciation” really follows one of the world’s great truths:

"It is better to give than to receive" (Acts 20:35). Truly, in the giving is the ultimate receiving.

I appreciate you caring about your organization and yourself enough to read and study this book. And I am grateful that you are committed to creating a healthy work environment.

Creative Opportunities

1. What is appreciation? What does it mean to you?
2. Define the methods of expressing appreciation that you like most to give—and receive. Be specific.
3. Look at the Lawrence Lindahl study. Make a list that includes all ten items in the study. Have everyone on the team (including executives) complete this exercise by ranking the list according to his or her personal opinion. Be honest. Don't put down what you think you "should" put down. Be real. Discuss. Determine actual ways appropriate rewards or expressions of appreciation can be provided. You can discuss

results as a group or individually, whichever way works best for you.

4. Describe how you feel when you work diligently on a project but no one says anything about your work—during the project or when it's completed. How does this affect your energy and enthusiasm for other projects?
5. Appreciation must be sincere. What does that statement mean to you?
6. Why is a chapter on appreciation included in a book about creating healthy work environments?

CHAPTER 15

Respect

I have no right, by anything I do or say, to demean a human being in his own eyes. What matters is not what I think of him; it is what he thinks of himself. To undermine a man's self-respect is a sin.
—Antoine de Saint Exupéry

When I interview team members and ask what they want most in the work environment, without a doubt, the number one thing people say is *respect. Webster* defines respect in the following manner: "a feeling of deep admiration for someone or something elicited by their abilities, qualities, or achievements." With this definition, can we agree that one earns respect—and it is not given freely?

Earned respect is a two-way street. Employees are vocal about the desire for respect, but employers also desire respect. In both cases, respect is earned.

How does one earn respect in the workplace? Here are seven ways to earn respect from the perspective of the employee and of the employer.

Seven Ways to Earn Respect in the Workplace

1. *Find out what is expected of you in your position and fulfill those expectations.*

Employee: If you have questions, ask! No one is going to think you are stupid for asking questions. Leaders will like your inquisitiveness and your desire to do things right. Make a commitment to do everything you do better than you even imagined possible. When you do all that is expected of you—and more—you will soar to the top.

Most people are happy to be average. But you're not (or you wouldn't be reading this book). So go for it! Tackle each responsibility with fervor and enthusiasm. Don't be afraid that other team members will think you are trying to win favor with the employer. (Although what's wrong with that?) Set the bar. You will become an asset to your organization. Managers will trust you with responsibilities. Do all that is expected of you and a little bit more—every time. You will soar. As Dr. Seuss said, "Oh, the places you'll go!"

Employer: Develop an excellent hiring process to make sure you hire the right team members. Both you and the interviewee should be able to tell whether this is a place or position that is best for them. Does it *fit*?

A good, updated job description includes the responsibilities of the position. Outline what you expect someone to do and how. Include the expected end results of each task. (See the chapter about accountability.)

Follow the adult-learning format I discussed in the chapter on integration. Remember that assumption is the lowest form of communication. Don't assume someone knows what you want. You are better off—and so is the new employee—to go overboard on training. Provide all that people need to know and a little bit more, at all times. Include a career-development program in your organization—one that is based on continuous education and skill development. This career-development program would include opportunities for personal development and communication training.

This type of program for continuous improvement is life giving to individuals, as well as to the organization as a whole.

2. *Be a continuous student. Learn. Be open to finding and implementing newer and better systems.*

Employee: Be a "forever student." Although there always seems to be a "goal" of getting out of school, perhaps a better mode of thought is to rejoice in never being out of school! There is so much to learn and so much knowledge to gain. School will never be *out* if you keep a dynamic mind-set of being a continuous learner.

Bring that mind-set and vivacity to the workplace. Be willing to continue to learn and improve your skills—and relish the opportunity. Your commitment to continuous improvement will set you apart from the average. Read, go to seminars, and take courses (online courses are available in almost every subject). You will be a continuous asset to your organization, and you will remain fresh, invigorated, current, and interesting.

Make a commitment to discover (or uncover) your talent.

Employer: Lead by example. Be on a "continuous path of improvement" (Deming, 1982). Apply this commitment to yourself and your own abilities and your organization. If you demonstrate a lack of desire to learn and improve, your team will immediately follow that same path, dooming your efforts. There is no such thing as status quo. You are either going up or going down. If you choose not to be on a continuous path of improvement, you are choosing to go downhill. This is true of any part of your life—and of the life of your organization.

Be willing to invest time and money in continuing education. The many methods of gaining education include courses, conventions, online seminars or webinars, audio instruction, consultations in your organization, and reading. Take a deep look at the various areas of your organization and ask yourself the following questions:

- What are we doing well?
- How can we do everything we are doing a little bit better?

Answer these questions honestly and seek out the teachers, coaches, courses, or whatever else it takes to gain the education you need for improvement.

3. *Be a leader of yourself and others by thinking ahead, by thinking outside the box, and by being an innovator.*

Employee: Listen to your inside voice, and when you have an idea, pay attention to it. Your ideas are worthy of consideration. Even the smallest and strangest ideas can be effective and productive. Think things through, but don't deflate yourself by thinking, *Oh, that's a stupid idea. No one will think that will work, No one will want to know what I think,* or *I just work here and do what I am told.*

Most employers are thrilled when a team member shows entrepreneurial spirit, enthusiasm, and interest in the betterment of the organization.

When you have an idea, think it through. Be prepared. Don't stifle yourself by analyzing your idea to death. Be willing to do what it takes to get your idea off the ground and running. When you do everything that is expected of you—and more—every time, you will rise to the top. Being average is not in your game plan. Being above average will earn you the ear of others.

Be positive about changes that will improve the practice or organization. Think of the possibilities of why something *can be done* and *can be helpful* rather than wallowing in thoughts of why something can't be done or won't work.

> I have learned, as a rule of thumb, never to ask whether you can do something. Say, instead, that you are doing it. Then fasten your seatbelt. The most remarkable things follow.
> —Julia Cameron, *The Artist's Way*

Employer: One of the responsibilities of being a leader is being a visionary. Vision focuses on the future. It's the clear picture of where the company is going.

> Any institution has to be organized so as to bring out the talent and capabilities within the organization; to encourage people to take initiative, give them a chance to show what they can do, and a scope within which to grow.
> —Peter Drucker

If creativity is not encouraged—or if a talented voice is not heard—the potential star becomes an eight-to-fiver—or the person leaves. They will come and do what they have to do, but no more. If stifled, they may become the doomsayers, the "gripers," the "carping skeptics" that James Belasco described in his book *Teaching the Elephant to Dance—The Manager's Guide to Empowering Change* (Belasco, 1991).

"Carping skeptics" find all the reasons something cannot be done. Their negativity can destroy energy—and a good project.

Fulfill your role as visionary. Encourage creativity and be an "idea seeker."

4. *Avoid the rut of doing things one way because it has always been that way. Take responsibility for innovation.*

Employee: It has been said that the definition of a rut is a grave with both ends cut out. Well, that may be a bit extreme, but the point is well made. If an employer/leader is a visionary and is following the mandate of that position to always focus on the future, change will be essential for staying on the forefront. Be careful not to fall into the category of "doomsayer" by getting stuck in a rut, unwilling to change. Honor the actions that have worked well, but be willing to move on when times and situations require. If you cannot embrace change and growth, you will either sap the energy of your colleagues or you will get left behind.

Change is hard because people overestimate the
value of what they have and underestimate the value
of what they may gain by giving that up.
—James Belasco, PhD

Jess Webber, MHA

President and CEO of The Jameson Group

Employer: "In a work environment, teams depend on each other to do their part. In a healthy work environment, everyone trusts each other to accomplish their responsibilities and, together, everyone moves the organization forward as a team of responsible adults working and trusting together. When you surpass the norm and work in a place where people can be trusted to contribute at a high level, an organization thrives and change becomes possible. While products, services, and delivery of services may change, the values of the company do not change." (Jess Webber)

5. *Work diligently to bring projects to a productive conclusion. Follow up and follow through. Make sure people can count on you to do the things you say you will do.*

Employee: As I said at the beginning of this chapter, respect is earned. People must be able to count on you. It's difficult to earn a person's trust, and it's easy to lose it. If people can't count on you to get things done in the proper time and manner, they will hesitate to give you projects or won't ask you to participate. Being given responsibility and then being trusted to fulfill that responsibility is a major motivator in the workplace. Build a reputation of accountability, and the path to growth will widen for you. Opportunities will be boundless.

Employer: A major frustration to employees is when their leaders put great ideas on the table, but nothing ever seems to happen. It's like crying wolf. Pretty soon, people stop listening. Also, negativity can set in.

For example, "I don't know why we have these meetings. Nothing ever happens. This is a waste of time. He won't do anything. He won't even remember that we had this discussion. So why do we even waste our time?"

Casting vision or proposing mandates to employees for projects without paying attention to the progress invites a lack of enthusiasm and commitment on their part. This is a sure way to lose respect.

Follow up and follow through. Don't be (or appear to be) too busy to pay attention. That's a fast way to show people that what they do doesn't matter.

6. *Recognize accomplishments and acknowledge people for them.*

Employee: Be genuine and generous with your compliments to your teammates and to your employer. I want your employer to recognize you and your work well done, but don't fail to thank your employers for your own opportunities. And thank your coworkers who participated in a project, gave a helping hand, or offered encouragement.

Be grateful. Say thank you.

Employer: When you recognize work well done, people are likely to repeat that behavior. If you want people to have the energy, focus, and desire to keep on doing good work, make note of it, recognize it, and give compliments. Remember the Dale Carnegie definition of a compliment: "A compliment is a statement of appreciation backed up by evidence."

- "John, you were right on time with that report on the ABC project. Thanks."
- "Jennifer, I appreciate your work on the XYZ project. The ideas were new and refreshing. You were really listening to our customers and altered that program to meet their needs—and ours. Good job."

Be grateful. Say thank you.

7. *Bring a positive attitude to each and every day. Leave your problems at the door and face your work with a sense of professionalism and grace.*

Employee and employer: I'll address this to both of you at the same time because it's exactly the same for all people in an organization.

Come to work focused on the business at hand. Of course you have problems and situations that dwell in your mind. Certainly, it is hard to focus on the business at hand when you have other issues that are begging for your attention. However, your colleagues and customers need your full, undivided attention. So compartmentalize. What's that, you may ask?

I learned the theory of *compartmentalization* from a hometown friend. After he graduated from college, he pursued his dream of flying jet aircraft for the United States Navy. He fulfilled his dream and flew an F-14 Tomcat. He was a hero!

When they were getting ready to land one of those amazing aircraft on the deck of an aircraft carrier (a very short runway)—in the daytime or in the nighttime—the pilot and the radio intercept officer (remember the two officers in the cockpit in *Top Gun*) would "compartmentalize." When you have important business at hand (in their case, landing the aircraft), focus completely on that task. If other thoughts come into your head, the distraction could compromise results—in their case, the safe landing—in your case, perhaps closing the sale, getting the job, completing a project, or listening accurately to a customer. Take the thoughts that are distracting you and put them in a closet in your mind. Close the door of the closet and lock that door. Focus on the business at hand. Then, when the time is appropriate, unlock the door and deal with your personal issue.

When you are at work, focus. Be there. Compartmentalize. The results of your productivity will increase immeasurably. And, on the flip side, when you are home with friends or family, do the same thing. Be there. Compartmentalize. Give your loved ones your undivided attention.

Compartmentalize. Focus. Do what you say you will do when you say you will do it. Treat others with respect, and that is what you will receive in return. Put up a mirror in front of your life. What you are receiving is a direct reflection of what you are putting out there. Be respectful to the people with whom you work, and they will reflect that respect back to you. *Respect* defines a company culture based on integrity and high standards. Respect is evident in organizations that are continuously creating and recreating healthy work environments.

Creative Opportunities

1. Ask members of your team to identify someone they respect. What about the person influenced your team members? What did they do? How did they treat others? What points of leadership were evident from them?
2. Have a discussion about *respect*. Read the definition offered in this chapter and discuss what the term means to members of the organization.

3. Review the seven ways to earn respect and discuss what you are doing to epitomize these principles. Pat yourselves on the back for the good things you are doing.
4. Ask yourselves where you could improve as a group. Be specific. Talk about the principle, giving examples of what is happening and how it could be better.
5. Have each person pinpoint one thing they are going to do to earn more respect and one thing they are going to do to give more respect to others.
6. Make a commitment to incorporate compartmentalization into your life.

CHAPTER 16

Accountability

I said, "Somebody should do something about that!"
And, then I realized I am somebody.
—Lily Tomlin

- I just don't know how to hold people accountable.
- People ought to know what they are supposed to do!
- But getting them to do it without me hovering over them is challenging.
- I don't want to micromanage, but what else can I do?

I had a conversation with a manager of a division of a large corporation, and she expressed the concerns listed above. There are many important factors in her statement:

- She understood the importance of counting on people to get things done in a certain way in a prescribed time frame.
- She didn't know how to hold people accountable.
- She *thought* people knew what they were supposed to do, but there was doubt in her statement.
- She didn't want to micromanage, but she was ultimately responsible for getting people to fulfill their roles.

- She made an honest statement about her inability to manage the behaviors of her team—and lead.
- She was frustrated to the point of anger.

Accountability is vital to an organization's productivity and smooth operation. Ideally, people hold themselves accountable by accepting the premise that they are leaders of themselves. However, knowing what needs to be done and getting things done can be two different things. On one hand, there is the project, and on the other hand, there are the people engineering the project. There are two sets of skills. Peter Drucker said, "You manage projects. You lead people" (2002). *Accountability* paves the way for completed projects.

What Is Accountability?

Webster defines accountability as "an obligation or willingness to accept responsibility for one's actions." Think of accountability as clear expectations and commitments that are honored and kept. In the chapter on respect, I mentioned that people must be able to count on you to do what you have said you would do in the agreed-upon time frame to earn respect. All people on the team need to ask, "Can people count on me to do what I say I will do?" An honest answer and evaluation of this question could prove to be very eye-opening. Are you accountable to yourself? To others? Really? All the time? If not, who are you choosing to let down?

If you are in a leadership or management position and have responsibility for people's ultimate results, you may want to pose these questions and have your teammates do their own self-analysis.

When accountability is part of the fabric of an organization, projects will be completed with fewer mistakes, delays, and deficiencies. Now, that will reduce stress!

Clear expectations. Kept promises. Accountability.

High Performance and Accountability Go Together

In their book, *Execution,* Ram Charan and Larry Bossidy (2002) studied Fortune 500 CEOs and asked, "Why do certain CEOs fail?" Their research determined the major reasons CEOs failed.

- inability to execute (thus the name of the book)
- inability to get things done
- inability to make decisions
- inability to follow up and follow through

We will look at this more intricately in the chapter on decision making, but we will also study this in the present chapter.

Each person is the CEO of him/herself. As the CEO of yourself, when you look at the list above, would you say that you are successful as your own CEO? If you have areas of weakness (and who doesn't?), once you identify those areas, you have taken the first step toward improvement. You don't fail if you learn from things that are not going well and do something about them. In fact, there is no such thing as failure—as long as you learn from each and every mistake. Learn how to do things better and how to be on that "continuous path of improvement," and then do it!

Failure doesn't mean you are a failure. It just
means you haven't succeeded yet.
—Robert Schuller

When you have a productive, positive attitude, choose not to wallow in self-pity or blame, and work at getting better, good things happen. It may be easy to say, "Oh, I just can't do that. That's the leader's job—not mine," rather than learning a new skill and constantly moving onward and upward. Dr. Ken Blanchard says, "You never hear 'that's not my job' on a high-performing team" (2000).

To truly be accountable to yourself or the members of your team, you have to walk the talk. When you say you will do something, do it. When there is a lack of continuity between what you say and what you do, teammates or clients will question your integrity. They will be afraid to trust you. You cannot say one thing and do another and earn trust or respect. What you say you will do and the actions you take must be congruent. I don't care if that means changing a lightbulb. If you said you would change that lightbulb today, do it.

Know in your heart that you are a person who can be trusted. You will feel so much better about yourself when you live in a place of honesty instead of deception. People can deceive themselves to the point where they actually believe they are right. It's so much easier to blame another person if things don't get done. It's so much more comfortable if a finger can be pointed at someone else. People think that putting other people down or blaming them will make the "blamer" look better, but nothing could be further from the truth. Although people may artificially declare themselves to be right by making excuses or blaming others, the ones who really lose are the ones who do the blaming. Continuously blaming others will deflate your sense of self-worth. There's no benefit to this. People will respect you when you are honest. Even if you don't know how to do something, make a mistake, or aren't as good as someone else, be honest about that. Seek training and education. Make a commitment to get better—and you will. Your colleagues will feel much better about you, and you will feel much better about yourself.

All blame is a waste of time. No matter how much fault you find with others—and regardless of how much you blame them—it will not change you. The only thing blame does is keep the focus off of you when you are looking for external reasons to explain your unhappiness or frustration. You may succeed in making others feel guilty about something by blaming them, but you won't succeed in changing whatever it is about you that is making you unhappy (Dyer, 1976).

Clear Expectations

Accountability depends on clear expectations. With clear expectations, people know what they are supposed to do, how they are supposed to do it, and when they are required to finish. In addition, a person needs to know the expected and required end results of any activity. Clear expectations need to be:

1. Visual. Write down the requirements of the job or project. Follow the adult learning criteria outlined in chapter 5 on integration. Approximately 83 percent of learning takes place visually; if someone is going to master a new skill, more visual instruction and teaching leads to better results.
2. Measurable. Clarify expected end results. How many new clients are needed from the recent marketing project? How many pieces of equipment need to be sold each month? How many clients will be contacted each week for customer-service surveys? Some projects will have clear, numerical measurements. Some may not. Monitor progress. People function better with clear goals and specific instructions. Measure results.
3. Clear understanding. Don't *assume* someone knows what he or she are supposed to do: be specific. Give clear directions and ask your colleague to repeat the instructions back to you to make sure they heard you accurately. A simple, but powerful description of good communication is "clear message sent—clear message received." It is impossible to fulfill a requirement or expectation without clarity. A person must know what to do,

how to do it, the deadline for completion, and the expected end results.

The least questioned assumptions are often the most questionable.
—Stephen R. Covey

4. Time specific. Set timelines and deadlines. Check in with people to make sure they are progressing. Alter time frames when and where appropriate (if there is mutual agreement). Be realistic with your time goals, but do not accept the ultimate destroyer of accountability: the excuse of "I don't have time." Good leaders organize their time so the top-priority activities and projects receive the necessary time for completion. Everyone has the same amount of time. Performance wanes when people become confused about priorities. Time becomes a destructive force rather than a constructive force. *The ultimate lack of accountability is the "I don't have time" syndrome* (see the chapter on delegation).

You may be disappointed in someone's performance, but before passing judgment, ask some questions: Have I been clear about what is to do be done? How it is to be done? Have I demonstrated, trained, observed, or coached? Have clear time parameters been defined and agreed upon? Are the expected end results understood? Are expectations clearly understood by both of us (or all of us, when appropriate)? The answers to these questions will guide the way to quality assurance for yourself and others. Remember not to make assumptions!

The only possible failure would be never managing to find the right role or the right partners to help you realize your strength.
—Donald O. Clifton

Areas for Clear Expectations

- Job Expectations
- Reward Expectations
- Communication Expectations
- Stress Expectations

Job Expectations: What is to be done? How? When? Goals? The more detailed you are with instructions, the better the results will be.

Reward Expectations: During your orientation and integration phase of employment, outline the salary, benefits, and any bonus programs you may have in place. If you have a bonus program, establish parameters related to the bonus. If you want a bonus program to work and truly motivate employees, you must clearly outline how the bonus works, calculate the bonus openly and honestly, and give bonus checks at the agreed-upon time.

Communication Expectations: Relationships of all kinds, including work relationships, are made or broken by the quality of the communication between or among people. Study. Constantly get better in this area of life! There will never be a day when anyone is a perfect communicator. There will always be room for improvement.

I've taught communication for many years and am passionate about it. However, I mess up situations and relationships! And when I look at situations that could have been handled better, the reason for the "mess up" is usually related to poor communication.

Be committed to looking deep within. When things are not going as well as you would like or if there are relationships you would like to improve, take a close look at your own communication. Start there.

- Do members of the organization know the communication channels?

- Do people know where they can go for instruction, honest conversations, questions, and concerns?
- Are you holding powerful, productive team meetings so people know what is going on? (You don't want people to find things out at the water cooler!)
- Do you invest in the study of communication skills for yourself and your team?
- Is there anything more important to the success of your business than communication skills? This lifelong study is worth your effort and attention.

Stress Expectations: Each person handles stress differently, and different situations affect different people in unique ways. What causes stress for one person may not cause stress for another, but you can do your best to outline timelines and deadlines, goals and expectations, "rules of the game," and expected interchanges between and among team members, including the executive team. Establish and update your communication channels so people are not blindsided by unexpected requirements or expectations. The more effective the systems of an organization, the better your stress will be controlled.

Accountability

Growth, productivity, and desired results come from the collective results of the entire team. No person on the team is any more important than any other member of the team. No one—not even the CEO—can function fully and effectively without every member of the team performing excellently. Poor performance or unreached goals are a collective failure—a shared failure. On the other hand, excellent outcomes are a collective and shared success—to be celebrated by all. This is joint accountability, which is a vital element for creating a healthy work environment.

Creative Opportunities

1. Discuss accountability. Start by reading *Webster*'s definition of accountability and build on that definition to make it resonate with you. Where do you see evidence of accountability in your organization? Where is it lacking? How can that be altered?
2. Do an internal inventory: Do you have current, clear job descriptions for each employee, including the executive team? Do they contain the following:
   - What is required of the position? What do you do?
   - How is each task to be performed?
   - What time frames are required for the completion of projects?
   - What are the expected end results? How are these results going to be measured?
3. Do you have clear channels of communication? Do the people on the team know what those channels are and how they work? Do they know who to go to for what? Are you assuming people know? Do they? Would an inventory of this during a specific team meeting be helpful? If so, schedule the meeting. Be open and honest.
4. The ultimate lack of accountability is the "I don't have time" syndrome. What does that mean to you and your team? Do you hear it? Do you say it? What are the time issues? Would a study of time management be helpful?
5. Conduct a survey of employees, including the executive team. Find out where people feel stress is overwhelming or out of control. Define the specific situations that are causing stress. One by one, work at refining those specific areas—or providing support or coaching for a division or a specific individual to reduce stress. Overwhelming stress saps energy and reduces productivity. Taking the time to work with employees to control stress will prove to be productive for the individuals and for the organization as a whole.

CHAPTER 17

Pride in Work Well Done

Life's most persistent and urgent question is
"What are you doing for others?"
—Martin Luther King Jr.

In my work with businesses large and small, I have found that one of the most energizing factors in a healthy organization is pride in work well done. In this reference to *pride*, I am not referring to the pride that is egotistical, but rather to the healthy "pride" of doing things well. When customers, clients, and patients receive excellent care and optimal results, team members feel good about themselves and about the results of their work. They are ambassadors for the organization. This healthy pride is evident in people who are serving others, making a difference, and focusing on purpose.

Clients and customers respond with loyalty when they receive this kind of dedicated care and attention. These loyal customers, clients, and patients become your greatest sales force. Jim Rohn said, "One customer well taken care of could be more valuable than $10,000 worth of advertising" (and that could be conservative!).

No matter what your job, your career, or your profession, perform with excellence. Be the best at whatever you are doing. Some people are satisfied with being average. Really? Who wants to be average? What does that ever gain? Where is the joy in that? Make a decision—no matter what your position or responsibilities—to do the best you can. Learn how to do things well, and do it every day, every chance you get. When you make a decision to be above average—and you perform in that manner with a positive attitude—you will soar. Average? No way! Be exceptional! By doing so, you will always be in demand in your organization or in the workforce. And you'll be much happier. When you are committed to performing with excellence, you'll feel better about yourself. A good feeling will fill your entire soul.

The way to find yourself is to lose yourself in the service of others.
—Gandhi

History

Each of us has a history. You do. I do. Everyone does. And a piece of that history is a work history. I've had many different jobs throughout my life. I'll bet you have too. My work life started with chores around the house, babysitting, ironing clothes, taking care of people's pets, working in retail, modeling clothes (that I couldn't afford to buy), filing documents in the library of my university, transcribing notes for a biology professor, teaching piano lessons, and many more. Once I graduated from college, I began my career as an elementary school teacher (which I loved). I had a singing career that involved recording and stage work. At the same time, I managed our horse operation and ranch. Over time, I held most every job possible in my husband's dental office. Now I enjoy a career as a professional speaker, management and leadership consultant, associate professor, and writer. I am grateful for each and every job and the experiences of each. My most important job is being a mother and grandmother!

I am thoroughly convinced that each and every job helped me prepare for whatever was next. I am grateful for each experience. No matter what I was doing, I tried to do the very best I could.

My parents taught my two brothers and me the value of honoring our employers and *always* doing the best we could at everything we did. I sometimes wonder about the white shirts I was ironing when I was thirteen! Did those corporate executives—friends of my parents—actually wear those shirts or take them from my ironing board straight to the professional cleaners? Maybe they were just supporting my entrepreneurial spirit as a young teen! Who knows?

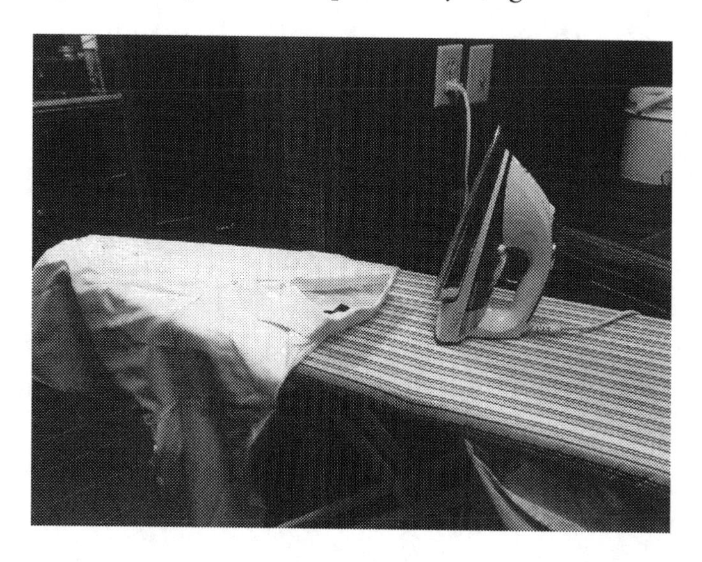

I imagine that resonates with you. You have probably had one job after another as you worked your way to your present life. You probably learned skills that are valuable to you today. You may have learned what you did not want to do for the rest of your life, which is a good thing to learn! Skills you gained, experiences you encountered, and people you worked with have all touched you. These are embedded in your DNA. You are who you are because of your genetics, your upbringing, your experiences, and the attitude you brought to each undertaking. No matter how large or small your job or task, it was vital and important to the whole. And it still is. If you undertake each task with a commitment to serve—and you look deeply into the value of your role—you will find an internal joy that no one else can give you. You find it yourself. Jessica Guidobono said, "Every job is a self-portrait of the person who did it. Autograph your work with excellence."

The Bricklayers

There is an age-old story about three men who were laying bricks. A passerby stopped and asked what they were doing. The first man said, "I'm laying bricks." The second man said, "I am putting up a wall." And the third man said, "I am building a cathedral." Simple—and powerful. All three men were doing the same thing, but their attitudes toward their work were significantly different. There is no single person on a team who is any more important than any other person on a team. Yes, there are differences in titles, positions, responsibilities, and compensation, but without each person on a team doing his or her part—and doing it well—the organization cannot "function at full capacity." The difference in the three bricklayers was their attitude.

Every day, each person has a choice to make about the attitude he/she will bring to the day—and to the workplace. William James, the father of psychology in the United States, said, "The greatest discovery of my generation is that a human being can alter his life by altering his attitude." The bricklayer who saw his role as a builder of a cathedral saw the bigger picture. Brick by brick, he was building a cathedral! Therefore, the placement of each brick was very important to the whole.

The principle behind this story is relevant today. Here is an example. I know a young woman who is a physician's assistant. She works with a superior surgeon. She is not the doctor. She is not performing the surgeries. However, her care of the patients, her management of the schedule, including hospital schedules, health histories, and medications, her physical assistance during surgeries, and her emotional support of the physician make it possible for him to "function at full capacity." Her role is imperative. Her attitude is positive, constructive, supportive, and loving. Without her functioning with excellence and competency, the surgeon would find it difficult to provide optimal care. Her role is vital. She makes it possible for the surgeon to do the things that only a surgeon can do. Her value is immeasurable. Her work and her role are part of each patient's successful surgery and recovery.

The same can be said about you—no matter your role, your position, your profession, or your industry. Your role is imperative to the whole. Focus on the bigger picture. Your organization needs you and cannot function optimally without you.

Are you laying bricks, putting up a wall, or building a cathedral?

Doing It Right the First Time

If you are like the third bricklayer, you understand that if you don't get a brick placed correctly, the stability of the cathedral is at risk. He isn't going to do that. He knows that each brick is essential to the final result. Over the centuries that follow, the parishioners of that church will be grateful that he did things right the first time. The results could be disastrous if he failed in his tasks.

How about the physician's assistant? Do you think her role is important? Do you think she should do things correctly the first time? If you are a patient there, do you want the surgery scheduled properly? Do you want appropriate radiographs so the doctor can do the right thing in the right way? Do you want the appropriate follow-up so your recovery is excellent and managed well? Of course. You don't want her to do things halfheartedly. You don't want her to make mistakes. It's your body! You want her to do things right the first time. Seconds are not acceptable!

As you are undertaking any task, consider the following:

1. Get your mind in the right place. Know that no matter how large or how small the task or responsibility may seem, it is important. Otherwise, you wouldn't be asked to do it.
2. Visualize what you need to do and the end results you are expected to accomplish. Buddha said, "The mind is everything. What you think you become." So think about success. Visualize doing things excellently.
3. If you are unclear about what you are to do—or if you feel inadequate—ask for help. People do not perform well if they don't know how to do something. Well, ask! If you are expected to do something well, make sure you have the skills and knowledge to do so.

   A word of encouragement here: there may be a time when you are competent at a new skill but lack the confidence to move out on your own. Well, sometimes, you just have to jump. However, do not hesitate to ask for feedback or evaluation of your work. When you perform a task—and your feedback is positive—you will be more confident the next time. Mastery of the skill will soon be yours.

4. Be sure to read any instructions that may be available to you. Whether you are studying the operating manual for a new computer system, reviewing the instructions for how to administer a new medication, reviewing the care of a different plant that has been placed in your greenhouse or nursery, or anything else, read the instructions! That could save you a lot of time, reduce mistakes, and prevent embarrassment when a customer asks a question and you have no clue!
5. Study. Go to courses. Enroll in online webinars. Read books. Study! There will never be a day when you know all there is to know about your subject—or any other subject. The world is always evolving, and new, relevant information is constantly being developed. Stay on the cutting edge or the world will

quickly leave you behind. This too will help you save time. You will be better able to do things right the first time.

Hall of Fame basketball coach John Wooden said, "If you don't have time to do it right, when will you have time to do it over?" Doing things right the first time is indicative of taking pride in work well done and is part of creating a healthy work environment.

Creative Opportunities

1. Take pride in work well done. What does that mean to each member of the team?
2. Have the members of your team (or division) identify which aspects of their roles bring them the most satisfaction. Have them identify how their roles are imperative to the whole.
3. Ask each person on the team to talk about "service to others." What does that mean? What services are you offering or providing in your organization? How do your products or services make a difference in the lives of your customers, clients, or patients? How does it feel to know that you can make a difference? Give specific examples.
4. Describe a time when something was not done correctly the first time. What was the impact on the client? The team member? The organization? On you! What could have prevented the mistake?
5. Study the five steps of doing it right the first time. Break into small groups and discuss specific ways each participant can implement those steps. What would be the benefits of committing to that process?

CHAPTER 18

Engagement

Your employees come first. And if you treat employees right, guess what? Your customers come back and that makes your shareholders happy. Start with employees and the rest follows from that.
—Herb Kelleher, cofounder and former
CEO of Southwest Airlines

Employee Engagement and Customer Engagement

What is engagement? Allegiance, a business-consulting firm, defines engagement as "the emotional bond or attachment that a customer develops during the repeated and ongoing interactions accumulated as a satisfied, loyal, and influencing customer." They continued, "Any discussion of engagement must include the relationship between the customer and the employees who are responsible for taking care of the brand."

When the leaders of a business inspire employees to function at a high level of excellence, many constructive results evolve: measurable growth for the business, longevity of employees, fewer sick days, absences, and tardiness, improved cooperation between and among team members, and a willingness to change when it's time.

For a long time, the mantra of business has been that "the customer is first!" Certainly without satisfied and loyal customers, a company does not stay in business. So *yes,* the customer is the reason for the business in the first place. However, without *engaged* employees, the customer will not be satisfied. In today's digital world, finding an alternative company or provider of service is easy. Trust is hard to establish, easy to lose, and even more difficult to regain. Engaged employees who create and retain customers are the heartbeat of any healthy organization.

In the competitive world of business today, having satisfied customers is no longer good enough. Dr. Ken Blanchard encourages the creation of *raving fans*: people who receive all they expect and a little bit more every time they have an encounter with the business (Blanchard, 1993). The goal of the organization is to move people from satisfied customers to faithful customers and then to engaged customers. Engagement is the key element of successful businesses in the twenty-first century.

Carrie Webber, Chief Communications Officer, The Jameson Group

Actions not words build trust. As a leader or as a teammate, knowing that others can believe you will do what you say

is integral in creating and supporting a high-performing team. It seems so simple. But you will often find it easier said than done. Internal trust of team members leads to trust from and with clients. This is the heart of engagement.
—Carrie Webber

"Having satisfied customers is no longer enough. You want people to receive all that they expect and a little bit more—at every contact. You want 'Raving Fans.'"

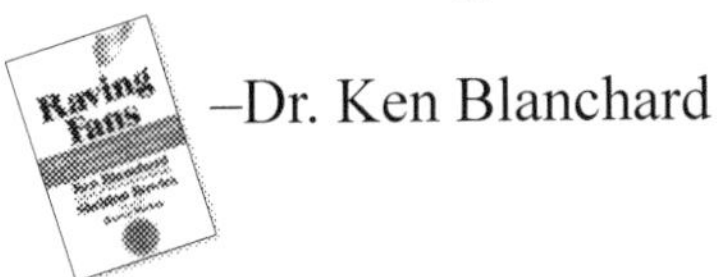

–Dr. Ken Blanchard

Engaged Employees

Why would an organization want to uplift its efforts to develop highly engaged employees?

1. Customer relationships with a company are often based on their interactions with team members. They may never see or speak to a member of the executive team. The team member *is* the organization from the perspective of the customer. A good encounter will create loyal customers, and the opposite is true. A bad or lackadaisical encounter will diminish the client's perception of the company as a whole.
2. The individual productivity of employees will translate to a more productive and profitable business.
3. There will be less turnover, which will reduce costs of staff changes and integration/training.

4. The better the service provided to customers, the higher the demand. The higher the demand and perceived value, the higher the fees that can be charged and received.
5. With a sophisticated, digitally savvy consumer population, organizations focused on highly engaged employees and customers will end up on top. People can easily choose who they spend their money with—and it might as well be you.

My Car Experience

When I decided to buy my first car (I was thirty-six), I knew exactly what I wanted: make, model, color, etc. I went to a well-known dealership by myself. They had exactly what I wanted. The salespeople were sitting in chairs along the showroom floor, but they didn't get up to give me the time of day.

Finally, a salesman came over to me and asked, "So, little lady, are you interested in a car?"

"Yes, I am," I answered.

"Well, is your husband with you?" he asked.

"No." I explored the car and asked questions. Then (since I travel every week) I asked to see the trunk space to make sure it was acceptable. "May I see the trunk?"

"Oh, I might have known that you'd want to see the trunk. I didn't think you would want to see the engine."

(Yes, I was biting my tongue!) I asked to see his manager, and when he arrived, I said, "I came here today to buy a car. I know exactly what I want. I was ready to write you a check for the full amount. But with the chauvinistic way I was treated today, I wouldn't invest one dime with your dealership. I'll take my money elsewhere."

The salesman did nothing to find out what I wanted and why. He judged me without knowing anything about me. He *assumed* that I could not make a decision about buying a car without my husband. This disengaged person caused me to be a disengaged customer. They lost thousands of dollars that day.

I went to another dealership in another city. There, I was treated with respect and courtesy. The salesman listened. Rather than criticizing me, he complimented me on how much I had prepared for this purchase and how much I knew. I bought the car that day—and paid in full. I asked to see his manager and raved about the salesman and his professional care. He was an engaged employee, and I became an engaged customer.

I have told thousands of people about Park Place Lexus in Plano, Texas, because that *engaged employee* took such good care of me at the time of the sale and for as long as I owned the car.

Would I buy another car from that dealership? Absolutely. Why? Those people epitomized engagement. They believed in their product. They understood excellent communication and customer service. They worked with me with no judgment—and with respect. I am quite confident that the "sales professional" from Park Place Lexus treated all his clients with equal respect. Did he make good money? I'm sure he did. Did he make money for the dealership? No doubt. Perhaps more importantly, he created *raving fans* who bought vehicles, stayed with them, and referred others. Now, that's how you build a sustainable business.

Promoting Engagement

1. The mission and vision—or culture—of the organization focuses on employee development and customer service. Without a team of people who support the values of the company, the focus will be on selling the product rather than on nurturing long-term, repetitive relationships with customers. You want to develop long-term clients rather than one-time clients. I was not going to buy a car every year, but I did go back to them for service for as long as I owned the car—and that involved a two-hour, one-way drive for me. It was worth it. I have been a forever customer of theirs because I have told so many people about them and have referred many people to their dealership. Engaged customers provide purchases, retention, and marketing by telling others about their good experiences with you. Care at this level moves potential clients into existing clients.
2. Reward people for engaging customers just as they are rewarded for the initial sale. Make retention a valuable and honored asset to the company. Reward people for *retention.*
3. Develop a culture dedicated to employee improvement and success. Customer success cannot happen without employee success.
4. Obtain feedback from customers and share it with employees. Don't do this once or twice a year; do this regularly. How long do you want to wait before you find out that something is wrong? How long do you want to wait to provide positive reinforcement for work well done?
5. Recognize and continue the things that are going well and alter the things that need improvement.
6. Use quantitative measurements to determine the impact of engagement—or the lack thereof. These monitors are available through numerous sources, including online. Find the source

that works best for you. Establish benchmarks or goals for your company and track those to make sure your systems and people are reaching them. If that is not happening, determine the source of the problem and implement problem-solving skills.

7. Use the *golden rule*: "Do unto others as you would have them do unto you." Treat your team members just as you would want them to treat you—and how you would want them to treat your customers/clients/patients. You can't be Attila the Hun to employees and then expect them to be kind to customers. Their treatment of clients will reflect the leadership.

What does customer engagement mean for your organization?

Customers leave companies in vast numbers every year. The organizations often do not know the reasons. Dr. Blanchard advises companies to be wary of customers saying that everything is "fine." Fine is a placid word that describes placid service. Customers will often tell you everything was "fine" just as they are getting ready to go elsewhere! Create raving fans!

1. They come to you in the appropriate numbers because of effective marketing, including referrals.
2. They purchase your product or service. They say yes to your recommendations.
3. They pay willingly because they perceive a fair exchange of value.
4. They schedule meetings, appointments, and phone calls, and they keep those appointments.
5. They stay actively involved with you in whatever way is appropriate for your business. They always stay in your hotels,

return to purchase new cars, use all of your banking services, or come to you for your dental or medical care.

6. They refer others to you confidently because of the service you provided—because of your *engaged* employees.

Engaged employees create and support engaged customers.

The Forbes Corporation determined that 84 percent of customers who leave a company do so because of poor service. In my car experience, it wasn't the product (the car) that caused me to leave! It was the poor customer service. I bought the very same car—from a group that was engaged and who lived by the oath of good customer service.

Retention

Marketing for new customers is imperative for a business. Retaining existing customers is equally important. Losing clients every year causes heartache, headaches, and enormous financial losses. Consider focusing as much time and attention on retention as you do on generating new business. Carlson Marketing determined through extensive research that "US companies lose 50 percent of their customers every five years. Yet just a 5 percent increase in customer retention can increase profits by nearly 100 percent."

What difference could it make to the bottom line, stress control, and the enjoyment of work if clients stayed with you, referred to you, complained less, and expressed enthusiasm for your work/service? That is the question. The answer is *engagement.*

Consider the following fundamentals to amplify engagement:

1. Provide products and services that exceed expectations. Provide *raving-fan* service during every encounter.

2. Be creative. Continue to develop up-to-date products and services that meet the ever-changing needs of new and existing clients. Be essential. Be dynamic. Continuously study your industry and survey your clients to find out what they need, how they want their services delivered, and how you could take even better care of them. Perform surveys for feedback (on your own or through a professional service). Digital programs that link to your software will often have survey capability. Check it out.
3. Listen to clients. Pay attention to what they say on the phone, in face-to-face conversations, and on surveys. Once you gain insights from the feedback, respond to it! Change (if necessary).
4. Track appropriate data that measures your benchmarks and the effectiveness of your people and systems. Don't guess about data. Be accurate.
5. Try not to become defensive if a customer gives difficult feedback. The truth may hurt, but positive change can come about when you face reality.

Engaged employees create engaged customers.

When you integrate the principles set forth in this book, you create engaged employees/team members. Engaged team members epitomize the following:

1. They are committed to the purpose and mission of the company and are on the same vision path as the owner/employer.
2. They have been included in the development of and support the strategic plan for the growth of the company (the goals).

3. They are respected and respectful. They trust the executive team. They know they will be honored as valuable assets to the company.
4. They are confident and competent in their skills and are encouraged to maximize talents and gifts.
5. They want and receive feedback on their performance and rewards for work well done, including recognition and appreciation.
6. They express their opinions without fear of reprimand if their opinions differ from those of others.
7. They are included and involved.
8. They are encouraged to engage. They know that engagement translates to engaged customers—and an executive team that is grateful for that commitment.

Engagement is a valuable part of creating healthy work environments.

Creative Opportunities

1. Have team members describe two situations in which they needed to purchase something. Have them think of a bad experience and a good experience.
2. Describe the bad experience. What was irritating? What happened that turned you away from the business?
3. Describe the good experience. What made it good? How did the people treat you? How did you feel? What made you decide to buy? Would you go back?
4. Were the people in the second situation engaged? What did that mean to you in that situation? What was the evidence of that engagement? What was your impression of the business itself? Did that impression reflect the members of the team?
5. Translate that to your own business. What can you do (or what are you already doing) to show engagement to customers?

What do you do that provides an excellent experience for your clients?

6. What does *engagement* mean to your organization? What can you do to promote and accelerate engagement? Write down one thing. Apply the goal-accomplishment system process (chapter 9-10) to that idea. Start now. Engage!

CHAPTER 19

Decision Making

Whenever you're making an important decision, first ask if it gets you closer to your goals or farther away. If the answer is closer, pull the trigger. If it's farther away, make a different choice. Conscious choice is a critical step in making your dreams a reality.
—Jillian Michaels

The knowledge worker today is interested in and capable of participating in company decisions. This participation will build capacity due to increased energy that erupts when employees are engaged. Of course, there will be times when the executives make solo decisions. However, as the workplace evolves into a more homogeneous environment, participation in decision making will be required.

Decision making and the impending results affect everyone. The more engaged people become, the greater their connection and interest in the organization's health. When people closely associate with one another and develop the ability to work compatibly and productively, they are interdependent (McLagan, 2003). Interdependence means that although individuals are motivated by accomplishments, they have an interest in the success of the whole. Employees become leaders when they clearly support others (Coy and Kovacs-Long, 2005).

A willingness to address problems and *work toward solutions* results directly from communicative ability. Communication is imperative *to making decisions* and helping employees gain decision-making skills, a cornerstone of effective leadership (McKnight, Ahmad, and Schroeder, 2001).

Decision Making: The "Why"

The *Business Dictionary* (2015) defines decision making as "the thought process of selecting a logical choice from available options." When trying to make a good decision, a person must weigh the positives and negatives of each option and consider all the alternatives. For effective decision making, a person must be able to forecast the outcome of each option and—based on all these items—determine which option is the best for that particular situation.

Makes sense. Sounds good. Then, why is decision making so difficult for so many people? And why is it one of the weakest areas of execution for leaders in the workplace today?

I have introduced you to the study by Ram Charan and Larry Bossidy (2002) related to why some CEOs are successful but others fail. Let's return to the list of the four dominant reasons.

Reasons CEOs Fail

- Poor Execution
- Not Getting Things
- Being Indecisive
- Not Delivering on Commitments

Excerpt from *Execution* by Larry Bossidy and Ram Charan

Do any of the four reasons cause us to fail (in a large or small project) or prevent us from reaching our goals and ultimate potential? Take a minute to think this through. Dig down deep for an honest answer that *could* be helpful.

People in leadership positions—which is all of you—are more productive when a *system* for decision making is instituted. A decision-making system? Yes! Emphatically, the answer is yes. Without a system for decision making, the following frustrations are expressed from employers and employees regarding this issue of "poor execution" or the "inability to get things done."

> Employee: "Oh, we go to these conventions or seminars and hear all this great information, but we come home—and life happens to us. Nothing ever changes. It's fun to go, but it doesn't really have any impact on what we do."

Employer: "I spend all this time and money taking people to courses, but they come home and fall right back into their routine. Nothing ever changes."

Blame Everywhere: The Decision Here Is to Do Nothing.

Employee: "I'm not sure why we have staff meetings. They're a waste of time. We come up with all these ideas, but we don't ever do anything with those ideas. We never follow up or follow through with anything."

Employer: "I don't know why I waste time and money on these staff meetings. No one even participates. I just spend an hour lecturing to the group. No one even acts interested. They say they want to do something, but they do nothing differently. This is a waste of time."

Blame Everywhere: Instead of Action

Employee: "Do something different? Isn't this company making enough money as it is? I can't do one more thing. I'm so busy I can't see straight. And, besides, it's working okay. Why should we do anything different?"

Employer: "These people need to do something, but I can't ask them to do this. They already have so many things on their plates. If I ask them to do one more thing—or make one more change—it would cause a mutiny. I want this to happen, but I can't possibly make these people mad or risk losing any of them. I guess things will just stay the same."

Blame in the Workplace

- People in the workplace tend to copy blaming as a behavior—consciously or unconsciously—thus perpetuating the problem.
- Conversely, when people see the leader taking responsibility, they copy that.
- Replace finger pointing with problem solving. Instead of thinking why something cannot happen, focus on how to move things forward.
- A culture of blaming leads people to be afraid to try something new. Stifling.

Some people cannot make decisions. That is one of the stimulants behind *blame*. Therefore, life and opportunities pass them by. If a decision is crying to be made, make it. Otherwise, people become discouraged, disappointed, and unmotivated. A decision to face any issue, including who does or does not stay on your team, is worth the effort and (sometimes) the pain.

I worked with a client whose young organization was thriving until an economic downturn hit his area. He was entrepreneurial and wanted to accelerate his knowledge of business and marketing to become even more technologically savvy so he could get and stay on the cutting edge of his profession. And he did so. As he was progressing on that path of growth and development, a great deal of change was taking place in his business.

One woman had been with him since the company opened its doors. She was a good person who had been faithful and loyal, and the owner held her in high regard and respected her. However, as he began to progress, she was less and less comfortable with what was being required of her. She hid behind paperwork and busyness so she could appear irreplaceable. She refused to integrate with the new processes. She would not participate in learning about new ideas and procedures. Progress stifled.

This young entrepreneur became stressed, discouraged, and sour. He didn't want to go to work, and that showed in all that he was—or was not—doing. He began to question himself. He knew that this long-term employee was becoming a stumbling block to his progress, his success, and probably to the survival of his business. Finally, he decided to release her.

When I asked him how he felt, he replied, "Well, that was one of the most difficult things I have ever done, but it was one of the best things I have ever done. I felt like a million pounds was lifted off my shoulders."

The other team members picked up the slack until a new, innovative, progressive person could be hired and integrated. The other team members also felt relief because they wanted to move forward, but they were constantly being pulled down by the recalcitrant employee. They were supportive of the change and stepped up to the plate. From that day forward, his business skyrocketed.

Blame Everywhere: The Decision Is to Retain the Status Quo.

> Employee: "Most of us on the team want to move forward, and we know we need to, but there are people (or a person) on the team who constantly hold us back. She's the ultimate doomsayer, but no matter how negative she is or how poorly she performs, he seems absolutely against letting her go or making a change in that position. We keep carrying the load for her."
>
> Employer: "I hired her, so I have to make this work." "I know that if I just get the right coach with her, things will begin to happen. I know that everyone's pretty frustrated, but I think she'll change." "If I let her go, people will get scared and think I'm going to let everyone go."

Blame Everywhere: The Decision Is Avoidance

Have you heard these kinds of comments? Have you made them yourself? Maybe not exactly—but translate the issues behind the comments into your own realm. I'm sure you will recognize situations.

Blame is the antithesis of execution. Blame is an excuse that validates behavior—even behavior that is less than productive. Blame stifles decision making. Blame is a decision unto itself; it suffocates the human spirit and the spirit of an organization.

Making Decisions

Decision making is not always easy, but it is an essential element for creating a healthy work environment.

The CEO of your organization must always make decisions that are good for the organization. Sometimes those decisions are unpopular, but he or she must make decisions that support the health of the company. Of course, that also means taking care of the people who make up the company: the executives, the employees, and the customers.

As the CEO of your own self, you will be making decisions every day. Decision making applies to each team member and is an intricate part of each person's role. The decisions you make about how you carry out your responsibilities will affect everyone in your organization.

Think about the number of decisions you make every day! Many! Every interaction with a client, a potential client, or a teammate involves making a decision.

Let me give one example:

If you are the one answering the phone, you have many decisions to make:

- How soon will I pick up the phone?
- What kind of energy will I put into this call?
- How will I handle questions proposed to me?
- What will I do with the information from the caller?
- Do I care if this person becomes (or remains) a client of our company? If so, does my handling of this call matter? Am I willing to do a good enough job to make a difference? And so on.

Create a line of questions for each person and each position in an organization. If you agree that each person in an organization is as important as every other person—and each person's role is imperative for the *healthy whole*—you can see the significance of each and every decision.

Owners and executives must make momentous decisions, including the following:

- Do we acquire this or that company?
- Are we prepared to access (or give) this kind of loan?
- Shall we expand into other states or countries?
- Shall we continue to employ this CEO or coach?
- Shall we make a change at this high level?

However, each person on the team makes decisions every day that attract or solidify more business or destroy business. This chapter is not only for executives of your organization; it is for each team member. It is for you.

Decision Making: The Process and the How

The following two figures succinctly list the steps of decision making, which are applicable to deciding where to go for dinner or deciding whether to buy a company. The amount of background study and the results of the decision will be altogether different, but the process is the same.

First, define the situation clearly. The more clearly you define the parameters of the situation at the outset, the more accurately you can direct your efforts. Proceed through each of the questions, moving from one question to the next in a succinct manner. Do a careful analysis, but don't get stuck. Moving too slowly or not moving at all is a decision in itself (perhaps not a good one). Make a decision.

Decision-Making *Process*

- ➢ Why is this decision necessary?
- ➢ Benefits?
- ➢ Challenges or "downsides"?
- ➢ Alternatives?
- ➢ Pros and cons of each alternative?
- ➢ Effect of each alternative on the company?

Guidelines for Effective Decision Making

- Set deadlines.
- Decide quickly on small issues and go on. Make the call.
- On larger decisions, make a series of small decisions that keep you moving forward.
- Once you come to a conclusion, have confidence in your decision.
- Don't back away from your responsibility.

If the entire team learns this process, things can happen! When team members know that decisions are made with intention and that a process for moving into action is in place, it elevates the entire organization. People move more quickly, taking actions and yielding results.

Effective decision making leads to results: getting things done, delivering on commitments, and executing. Execution makes a big difference and is an imperative component for creating a healthy work environment.

Creative Opportunities

1. Do a survey of your own decision-making capability. Ask yourself the following questions:
   - Do I have the confidence to make decisions? If not, what are my major hurdles or barriers?
   - Once a decision is made, do I follow through to ensure the decision is executed appropriately? Do people know that I expect completion of tasks assigned to each particular person (including myself)?
   - Can and do people come to me confidently when they are reporting on progress or reporting on difficulties? If we have a snag in the process, are we working through it—or are we getting stuck and not moving forward?
   - Do all people involved in the action plan concur with the decision? Have I presented it well enough so they commit? Are there clear expectations of necessary actions and anticipated results? Is there a coordinated plan for following up and evaluating? If we need to make changes, are we willing and able to make those changes? And do we?
2. Identify one decision that has not been made yet. Write down the issue. Review the decision-making process presented in

this chapter and walk through as many steps as possible. Note any areas that need further study or opinions—and make a plan to do just that.

3. If you are prepared to make the decision and you believe it will benefit your workplace, pull the trigger.
4. Reread this chapter on decision making and incorporate these processes in all areas of your organization. You will move forward. You will see results. You will get things done. You will be able to fulfill commitments. You will be able to execute. Make it happen!

CHAPTER 20

Confrontation with Care

If you find yourself in a confrontation of any kind with anyone, before reacting ask yourself, is what I am about to say motivated by my need to be right or my desire to be kind? Then, pick a response that stems from kindness, regardless of how your ego objects.
—Dr. Wayne Dyer

Confrontation! Oh how we hate the thought of this word and what it means! Most people avoid confrontation at all costs! People avoid confrontation for many reasons, many of which are related to fear:

- of hurting another person
- that the other person will get mad or leave (or both)
- that more problems could be created

People (for the most part) want loving, caring relationships with family, friends, colleagues, patients/clients, etc. People don't want others to be upset with them, dislike (or hate) them, or show disdain. Rather than running that risk, they avoid confrontation.

This does not mean that avoiding a problem makes it go away. Nor does this mean there are no problems. Oh, no. Everyone has problems. Every organization has problems. But the difference between being successful and not is being able and willing to face and solve those problems.

Confrontation with Care?

Confrontation? Care? How can these two words be placed together in the same sentence? Is that possible? Confrontation means fighting, anger, quarreling, doesn't it?

Not really. Of course, confrontation *can* lead to disharmony and can hurt if it is not done well. Most people avoid or shun confrontation because they have had such difficult or hurtful experiences when they confront someone or when someone confronts them! Communication is based on skills and can be learned and continuously improved. Constructive confrontation is part of the skill set called communication: a clear message sent and a clear message received.

When people are afraid to confront, and avoid doing so, it's often because they have never been taught the skills of how to confront with care. Some people handle conflict like ostriches—they stick their heads in the sand and pretend they don't see anything. They deny the problem, hoping it will just go away. People think if they don't acknowledge something, it must not be there.

Other people avoid conflicts or confrontations by meeting teammates in the staff lounge, at the water cooler, or in the sterilization area to gripe about other people, the boss, and the way things are going. Now, that's effective! That's a great way to solve a problem! Drag everyone else into the gripe session—pull them down—and wait to see if things get better!

> It's human nature to gripe, but I'm going
> ahead and doing the best I can.
> —Elvis Presley

With anyone in your life—kids, spouses, significant others, colleagues, friends—if you have a problem, it is important to address specific behavior that is causing a problem for you without being judgmental. Describe the behavior or situation that is causing you a problem, how it is affecting you, and the way you feel about it. It's important that the other person knows that you may not like what he or she is doing—but that does not mean you do not like the person. This is critical for all parents!

Confrontation with care means that something is bothering you—or downright upsetting you—–and you have asked yourself, "Is what this person doing having a concrete, negative effect on me, my performance, or the organization?" Your answer to that question determines how you proceed.

1. I don't really know. I'm not sure. I guess not. If this is your answer to the question, do one of the best stress-relieving things you will ever do: let it go! Do not wallow or stew over things that are not truly a problem.
2. But if you answered yes, you have (or own) a problem and have the right and the responsibility to address it. If you have determined that you have a problem, move into confrontation with a caring attitude and a commitment to finding a solution that works for both (or all) parties. Move forward!

Open the conversation about a problem—or initiate the confrontation—by sending what Dr. Thomas Gordon (2009) called an "I Message." This is a statement of the problem, how you feel about the situation, and the concrete, negative effect the person's behavior is having on you.

> Sarah, when you come to work fifteen minutes late, it compromises the quality of our morning meeting. We agreed on the value of these meetings in supporting a smooth, flowing day and assuring excellent care of our clients. Since you aren't there on time, the

> other team members have to fill you in. That takes much of their time and attention, which needs to be focused on clients. I'm really disappointed about this tardiness.

There is no judgment here, but there is a specific definition of the problem: the effect of Sarah's behavior on clients, teammates, and the company, and the feelings related to the situation. This is the beginning of confrontation with care, which opens the door for diplomatic problem solving.

Isn't there risk in confronting someone about a problem? Of course. The person may not take it well. You could make it worse by addressing it, especially if you address it poorly. That's why the communication skills in constructive confrontation are so important. Ignoring a problem will not make it go away, but confronting an issue poorly can lead to misunderstandings, further disagreements, and greater problems.

Think of *risk* as a two-sided coin. On one side of the risk coin is the chance that you might make a mistake. If so, learn from it and grow. On the other side of the risk coin is ultimate success. If you are never willing to risk, you can never experience life or relationships to the fullest. If you build relationships of trust and confidence, you will be able to weather most conflicts.

Not confronting an issue could put the relationship at irreconcilable risk. The risks of not addressing a problem are stressful, debilitating, and costly to the business.

- You can get more irritated.
- Poor performance or negative behavior could make other team members think you don't really care. If so, why should they care?
- Your relationship could deteriorate to a place that is irreconcilable.

If you recognize a problem, you have a chance to address it and (hopefully) solve it.

> We cannot solve life's problems except by solving them.
> —M. Scott Peck

Conflict in the Workplace

People often react or respond to conflict with one of the following stances, according to Dr. Thomas Gordon (2009):

- Aggressive: Control—trying to get people to alter their behavior through fear or guilt
- Nonassertive: Compliance—going along with whatever someone wants, in order to get along—no matter what
- Passive-Aggressive: Noncompliance—purposely trying to resist doing what is desired, or
- Assertive: Working together—finding a satisfying and acceptable solution

Although there are times when each of these responses may be appropriate, assertive behavior is most desirable.

What does that mean? Being assertive means being willing to speak your truth in a caring manner. The key to problem solving is to identify the needs of both people and work together to find an acceptable solution.

When things are going well, it is easy to get along with others. However, when people do things you don't like, you can handle the situation in several different ways.

- You may give in to keep the peace. However, when unacceptable behavior is allowed to continue, the relationship can erode. It can lead to alienation and unhappiness.

- You may become defensive, which usually adds fuel to the fire.
- You may harbor negative thoughts and feelings toward the other person, which can put a wall between the two of you—and the other person may not even know why!
- You can learn the skills of problem solving and confront your concerns from a place of care. This is the healthiest option!

The first three options are not helpful. You may think that giving in is loving behavior or that you should forget your own needs to meet the needs of the other person. From time to time, that is fine, especially if it doesn't cause a problem for you. However, if you do this all the time and continuously postpone your needs, you will eventually resent the other person. This is, of course, not the goal, and it doesn't help anyone.

In problematic or conflicting situations, you can choose either to deny there is a problem and hope it goes away (this too shall pass) or learn from the situation by working through the problem. Deny or learn. These are your options.

One of the most loving things you can do is express truth and honesty—no matter how difficult this may be. Most people want to do things correctly. They want to please their teammates or employers. They want to know if they need to improve—or if they are doing something wrong. You don't do anyone a favor by not addressing something that needs to be corrected. People care. If they don't care, then someone has a problem, but that person may not be you. If a relationship is built on trust, you can be secure in knowing that neither person would ever purposefully do or say anything to hurt the other.

If someone confronts you with a problem—something that is having a concrete, negative effect on them—try not to become defensive. It may be your natural reaction to become defensive.

However, when someone becomes defensive, the lines of communication are barricaded.

Solutions aren't often discovered when defensiveness infiltrates conversations. However, this is much easier said than done. Human beings often become defensive as a protective measure, but when the reaction is protective or defensive, nothing is learned—and problem solving becomes difficult (if not impossible).

When the mind and heart are open to meaningful, productive discussions, the result is growth. Think of *confrontation* as a gift you give yourself and others in an effort to move the relationship forward.

We'll look more intricately at the problem-solving steps in the next chapter. Confrontation with care is worthy of study and is part of creating a healthy work environment.

Creative Opportunities

1. Discuss the principles behind confronting with care. Why is this a valuable skill for a company and the people in it?
2. What is frightening about implementing confrontation with care?
3. Identify a situation where something someone is doing is having a concrete, negative impact on you, your performance, or your practice/business/home. Write a statement about the situation—and be very careful to write about the situation without being judgmental about the other person.
4. Write out an "I message" that describes the situation, the feeling that it generates within you, and the impact of that behavior.
5. After you study the chapter about problem solving, decide if you are ready to address the problem. If so, write out an "I message" that will start the conversation.
6. Write down one step you will take to turn a conflict into a healthier relationship through caring communication.

CHAPTER 21

Problem Solving: The Key to Progress

We can't create a new future while we're living
in the past. It's simply impossible.
—Joe Dispenza

We considered the value of confrontation with care in the last chapter. Some would say that the idea of confrontation being an act of care is unique. How can we confront someone about an issue or a problem without hurting feelings, causing more problems, or getting in trouble? The answer comes from the ability to communicate effectively. From this vantage point, confrontation becomes a gift you give to another person—and to your organization. Problem solving can be a gift that leads to improved relationships and improved productivity.

Einstein said, "We cannot solve our problems with the same thinking we used when we created them." Begin to look at challenging situations with an open mind, a creative perspective, and a positive attitude. Solutions can lead to unexpected answers.

Effective problem solving is based on a sincere interest in the issue or person and an emphatic desire to develop a solution. The key to progress and unseen opportunities is the ability to identify, face, and overcome problems. A problem that is left alone becomes a habit, but a problem approached with a new, fresh, creative mind-set can open the door for new ideas. New ideas can open the door to brilliance.

When you are face to face with a difficulty,
you are up against a discovery.
—Lord Kelvin

Problem solving has a negative connotation for many people (much like confrontation). However, if you turn that thinking around, you will realize that some of the greatest discoveries and advances in many fields came about when something went haywire and a person or group pooled their thoughts, ideas, and creativity to find a new and better way. Stories of that kind of revolution are endless.

Historically, every major scientific breakthrough began with a simple idea that threatened to overturn all of our beliefs. The idea that the earth was round was mocked as utterly impossible because most people believed the oceans would flow off the planet. Small minds have always lashed out at what they don't understand.

There are those who create—and those who tear down. That dynamic has always existed, but the creators eventually find believers. When the number of believers reaches a critical mass, the world becomes round. Perception is transformed, and a new reality is born (Dan Brown).

What is a problem?

Merriam-Webster took a traditional look at the word *problem*.

- something that is difficult to deal with
- something that is a source of trouble, worry, etc.
- difficulty in understanding something
- a feeling of not liking or wanting to do something.

The Free Dictionary offered a more constructive look at the definition of *problem:* "A problem is a question to be considered, solved, or answered. A situation that needs attention."

Einstein said, "Stop talking about your problems and start thinking about solutions." He was telling us that wallowing in our discomfort would do nothing to move us toward progress. Identify the problem—and proactively create a solution.

Microsoft eliminated the word *problem* from its company vocabulary. Rather, they address *issues* that are worthy of thought, creativity, and development—and the rest is history!

The human mind is indescribably capable. The potential within each person is immeasurable and (for the most part) untapped. Therefore, identifying a *problem* or *issue* and opening the mind to its creative potential can lead to untapped productivity and insights.

How do you go about solving problems constructively? Let's look at the process of problem solving. Individualize the steps to fit your situation and your particular needs.

Step 1: Define the problem.

1. State the problem. What is happening? What is working? What is not working? What is causing distress?
2. What expectations are unfulfilled?
3. What barriers are preventing you or the organization from reaching predetermined goals?
4. What is having a concrete, negative impact on you or your company?
5. Determine the cause of the problem. Identify the symptoms, but do not get stuck there. Move on.
6. Identify the problem in terms of the needs of all parties. Don't move on to finding a solution until you have clearly defined the needs. The needs of all parties must be met. If this does not happen, the solution may not work.

The definition of the problem may be the most important step you take in problem solving. As you are defining the problem, consider these questions:

1. What is the problem?
2. Is it mine? Is something having a concrete, negative effect on me, my performance, my division, or my company? Am *I* the problem?
3. Is this really a problem? Could we get good results if we followed a new idea or developed a new way of doing things? If so, how do we move forward?
4. If I determine that this is truly a problem, can I solve it by myself? Do I need help from others?
5. Am I focusing on a symptom rather than the actual problem? If so, can we dig deeper and find the root of the problem?
6. Is this worth solving?
7. Are we implementing solutions but the problem remains? If so, let's not keep doing what we are doing! Let's find another solution. Einstein said, "Insanity is doing the same thing over and over again and expecting a different result."
8. Will this go away on its own? (Be careful here! Avoid the ostrich syndrome.)
9. Is this a problem that needs immediate attention—or can it wait?
10. Can I risk ignoring this? What would be the downside of avoiding or ignoring this? Have I truly determined that there is no concrete, negative impact? If so, I can let this go!

Step 2: Generate alternative solutions.

1. Who needs to be involved? Stakeholders? Shareholders? Department managers? Directors? All team members?
2. What facts are identifiable?
3. Is there available research that would help with our decision?

4. Do we need to contact experts in this field to gain insights and recommendations? If so, who are the potential consultants? How will we evaluate their relevance to our situation?
5. What have we observed in the present situation? What have we observed in the past?
6. Where are we now? Where do we want to go? How are we going to get there?
7. What are the boundaries or parameters within which a decision can be made?
8. What are the realities? The biases? The opinions?

Step 3: Discuss the pros and cons of each alternative solution.

If there are too many cons, that idea may not work.

Step 4: Come to a consensus about the best solution (or solutions).

Step 5: Devise a plan of action for implementation.

1. Go back to the chapter on goal accomplishment and apply the steps outlined in that chapter. They are applicable here. A refresher may be helpful:
   - Write the goal. Be specific. Write the goal in the affirmative (as if it has already happened).
   - Design a plan of action: What will you do? How? Why is each step important? What are the barriers that need to be eliminated? What resources do you need?
   - Who will do what?
   - By when?
   - How will you evaluate progress?

2. Once you have a plan of action in place, just do it!

Step 6: Implement the plan,

Step 7: Evaluate!

1. Once you have put your plan of action into effect, evaluate your progress. Check in with the people involved. What do they think? How are they doing? How is the plan of action working? Do they have what they need to progress? If participants are having difficulty or are not pleased with the plan, listen to them. Give people the autonomy and trust to recommend changes. Be willing to change when and where necessary or appropriate. Don't keep on doing things that aren't working or aren't getting good results.
2. As you are evaluating your progress, be sure to celebrate the victories along the way! Don't wait until the project is completed to give people feedback. Give people recognition, support, and pats on the back for each step taken. Lao Tzu (Tao Te Ching) said, "A journey of a thousand miles starts with a single step." Celebrate each step.

The Key to Progress

At the beginning of this chapter, I said, "A problem approached with a new, fresh, creative mind-set can be the "key to progress." A new idea can become the door to opportunity, growth, and improvement. Look at problems and face them head-on. Find solutions. On the other side of a solved problem, you'll find strength, wisdom, and peace. Those are vital elements of creating a healthy work environment.

Creative Opportunities

1. Write down one unsolved problem you have at the present time. Be specific. Address the issue without being judgmental

or derogatory about an individual. (You may be having a problem with a certain person, but address the behavior instead of the person.)

2. Go through the steps of problem solving outlined in this chapter and ask yourself the questions as you work on the problem you wrote down.
3. If you determine that it is truly a problem—something that is having a concrete, negative effect on you, your performance, your division, or the company—decide whether you can work on this yourself or if you need help. If there are others who need to be involved, identify who they are and ask them to work with you.
4. Go through the stages of *implementation* and design a plan of action that you are willing and enthusiastic to activate (using the goal sheet from chapter 10 on goal accomplishment.)
5. Put the plan into action
6. Evaluate your progress.
7. Celebrate the small victories along the way.

CHAPTER 22

Delegation of Responsibility

If you delegate tasks, you create followers. If you
delegate authority, you create leaders.
—Craig Groeschel

Delegation of responsibility is one of the most profound motivators in the workplace. Appropriate and respected transfer of responsibility provides an acknowledgement of ability or skill mastery, an opportunity to grow, respect of and for talent, trust given through upgraded authority, validation (which builds self-esteem), and exciting challenges.

A challenge gives us greater diversity once accomplished.
From this comes a broader base of understanding and
creativity for the business and for ourselves.
—Dr. John Jameson

Steps toward Successful Delegation

No matter what your role in the organization, as you mature in your skills and stretch to the next level, delegation will be an attribute of your leadership (to yourself and your colleagues). As with all systems, there is a healthy way to handle delegation. Consider these proven parameters of effective delegation:

Know the benefits.

1. Stress relief. Delegation allows for the transferring of certain responsibilities, allowing everyone to focus on newly developed skills or other areas of the business that need attention. Prioritization can become a reality. Delegation provides stress relief because it prevents boredom, the sense of having "no place to grow," and feeling stuck.
2. Time management: Delegation lets you focus time and attention on the highest and most productive areas of your position. Make sure you (and everyone in your organization) are doing the things that are the most productive at all times.
3. Empowerment: A person who has developed and refined skills will be motivated to expand his or her expertise and be trusted with advanced responsibilities. The more knowledgeable and motivated the team, the more you can delegate.
4. Productivity: Align each person's responsibilities so they are doing the things that only they can do (including you). When each person becomes more productive individually, it translates to greater productivity for the business.
5. Life balance: Delegation lets people focus on what they do best—and where they are most productive. Done well, this prevents overload from tedious tasks that could be assigned elsewhere. When people have too much on their plates and cannot do anything completely, it subtracts from productivity, increases stress, and saps energy. People need to have plenty of energy to fulfill their roles at work and at home.

Things to Remember When Delegating

- Be sensitive.
- Match expectations to abilities.
- Give clear directions and expectations.
- Expect a person to work independently to get the job done.
- Ask people to "batch" their questions.
- Assign acceptable due dates.
- Monitor progress, but don't hover.
- Follow-up and evaluate.
- Give feedback.
- Say thanks.

Barriers and Obstacles

Will there be barriers and obstacles to delegation? Yes. Some will come from the person who is doing the delegating, and others will come from the person who is receiving the new assignment. Let's look at some of these obstacles.

1. Risk: You may run the risk of someone not doing things just like you do! Ouch! That hurts, especially if the results are phenomenal! On the other hand, the results may not be good at all. If not, step back, reeducate, and retrain. Define the obstacles and work to overcome them. Give the person chance after chance to be successful. Celebrate the small victories along the way. You'll see growth. Be watching. Pay attention.

2. Your Own Self: You may be the biggest barrier to delegation. There may be tapes playing in your head that prevent effective delegation.
    - "Oh, I can just do this myself."
    - "I can do this faster."
    - "It just takes me a few minutes."
    - "It's easier to do this myself than to teach someone to do this."
    - "If I have them do this, I won't be absolutely sure how it's done or if it's done right." (Loss of control)
    - "Yeah, but if they do it, the boss will give them the credit for this project—and I'm the one who is really getting things done." (Fear that someone else will get the credit)
    - Listen for your own internal tapes and ask, "Am I really the only person who can do this? If this responsibility were delegated, could that help me (or us) be more energetic, focused, and productive? Okay, yes. How can I get out of my own way—and the way of progress?"
3. Let Go: When you see that someone has mastered a new skill or responsibility and that the results are acceptable (or stellar), let go. Do not hold onto things once you have turned them over. Certainly, you can check in—give feedback, reinforce, give pats on the back—but don't take it back. If you do, you will undermine their self-esteem. Their confidence in trying anything new or taking on any new responsibilities will diminish. Their trust in themselves (and in you) will be compromised.
4. Give Up the Guilt Trip. There are many great trips to take in life, but a guilt trip is not one of them. If you have determined that you need more time to focus on productive aspects of your job and people on your team are willing and able to take on new responsibility, give them a chance. Once you have done so—and they are doing well—let go. Do so with joy.

> Recognize that you have given them a chance to grow and become better than they imagined. They feel better about themselves. They are on an upward path. That's a good place to go.

Don't feel guilty. Watch your internal conversations: "I can't ask them to do that. They will think I am a slacker." No, they won't! If you handle the situation with grace and respect, the transfer or delegation of a responsibility will be a statement of confidence. You will be showing trust that acknowledges their ability, stature, and capability.

Consider the benefits of effective delegation as outlined in this chapter. The advantages far outweigh the disadvantages. Create a win-win situation where talent and strength are maximized. Follow the system. Handle with care. Remember that people are motivated when they are trusted with responsibilities. Delegation is a vital component of transformational leadership.

The solutions and guidelines for effective delegation should look familiar. Pull all the learning we have shared into this process.

Dr. Joan Borysenko guides us by saying, "Patience is peace. Learning to be patient is a continual practice that takes years to ripen. Let it unfold, day by day, and be gentle with yourself in the learning."

Principles of Delegation

1. Delegate unless you are truly the only one who can do something.
2. Contemplate the positives and the negatives if something isn't done just the way you would do it.
3. Give up control once you are confident in someone's ability.
4. Share the credit.
5. Let go!

In *Creating a Healthy Work Environment*, the development of skills and the nurturing of talent are vital strategies. These strategies are good for people and good for organizations. Contemplate the benefits of delegation and apply the principles of how to make that happen.

Creative Opportunities

1. Make a list of the tasks and responsibilities in your job description at the present time.
2. Beside each item on that list mark them between one and five. One means the most productive parts of your role (things you do that make the most difference). Continue through each item, placing a number beside it. One is the most productive, and five is the least productive. This is not to say that everything on the list is not important or that each thing does not need to be done.
3. Now look at the fours and fives. Ask yourself—or your supervisor—if the items could be refined to be more efficient, lending more time to focus on the more productive items? Could they be eliminated? Do you still need to be doing this? Could they be delegated? If delegation is the answer, identify a person who has the ability or the desire to learn (or both). Follow the path in the graphs in this chapter to gain a person's interest and permission in accepting the new responsibility. Then begin the training process.
4. Once someone has taken over one of your responsibilities, make sure you focus the additional time and energy on the other tasks or projects that lead to improved productivity.
5. Let go. You will find that the other person's enjoyment of work will increase—and so will yours.

CHAPTER 23

Reward for Work Well Done

Start with good people, lay out the rules, communicate
with your employees, motivate them, and reward them.
If you do all those things effectively, you can't miss.
—Lee Iacocca

Appreciation is the strongest motivator of people in the workplace (and anywhere else, for that matter). Refer to the Lawrence Lindahl study, which continues to be reproduced in today's workplace with similar results. Notice how the factors that are motivational to people have remained the same throughout time. They are true as you read this book.

For employees, appreciation remains the strongest and most important motivator. It is followed by being recognized and acknowledged for work that has been done—and for work that will be done in the future.

In addition to appreciation, it is imperative that compensation be commensurate with the work and the contribution. If a work environment is going to be healthy, care and attention to employee emotional, physical, and financial health must be provided. Remember to use compliments and cash!

Let's look at rewards for work well done—in addition to appreciation.

Money won't create success, the freedom to make it will.
—Nelson Mandela

If employees don't have their basic needs met—safety and security—there is no way they can climb the ladder of improvement and higher productivity. If employees aren't maximizing productivity, neither can the organization. Healthy, productive, engaged employees lead to healthy businesses. Of course, if the company isn't productive and profitable, it cannot stay in business (as has been mentioned!). No one wins if no one has a job! It takes everyone working together—cohesively—to make things work and work well.

What does the research say?

As you create a healthy work environment, appropriate compensation matters. Again, referring to Maslow's hierarchy, a person has to feel safe and secure before he or she can expand and elevate to higher levels of growth and development. A person cannot move up the ladder of expertise, confidence, and improvement if the lower levels of need are not satisfied.

If people don't know if they are going to be able to pay the rent, buy healthy food for their families, put gas in their cars, or fund their kid's college educations, it is hard to strive for advancement. It's also hard for them to risk stepping out of their comfort zones to try new and different ways of working. If the comfort zone feels stable, stepping out of that space can be frightening and threatening.

Money isn't the most important thing in life, but it's reasonably close to oxygen on the "gotta have it" scale.
—Zig Ziglar

Financial rewards are not the major motivator of people in the workplace, but they still need attention. Leaders must organize compensation packages around the fulfillment of the mission of the company and the fulfillment of employee needs (Chaney, 2004). Only then will the issue of compensation add to—rather than detract from—productivity.

In the past, companies gave annual raises. This led to people feeling entitled to those raises even when performance and productivity had not improved. This was not good for the health of companies; in the long run, it was not healthy for the employees. (Note: if you are doing annual or semiannual performance reviews, a salary review is a separate appointment from the performance review.)

In contrast, Smilko and Van Neck (2004) found that if people went above and beyond expectations but *were not* compensated for outstanding performance, their productivity could go down. They became discouraged and thought, *Oh well, it doesn't make any difference whether I do a great job or not.*

When people do exceptional jobs and the company thrives, but there is no financial reward for their work well done, they can lose momentum. Compensation needs to be a win–win situation. When work is well done and the company benefits, the people who are responsible for that improvement must benefit as well.

Physical rewards that are applied to certain performance measures may provide short-term positive results, but they can lead to negative results if destructive competition results. Deterioration of productivity and a reduction in intrinsic motivation may result. Intrinsic motivators (earned respect, trust, responsibility, self-regulation, and clear, precise goals) are more effective. Teamwork deteriorates when people are engulfed in negative emotions about money. Jealousy, backbiting, and undermining can occur. Leaders must try to set a tone where people support one another's growth—and do not resent it. (This is tough to do, but it is worth the effort!)

The Relationship between Compensation and Productivity

Salary and compensation are imperative, of course. People have to be paid for the work they do. Some people say, "I love my work so much that I would do it for no pay." That's great, but the truth is that it takes money to survive and thrive in the world today—and to take care of family needs.

Salary is important, but it becomes a "demotivator" when the employer gives the paycheck to the employee in a negative manner—or when a well-deserved raise, bonus, or commission is given with resentment or the salary structure is unfair (or inappropriate). Salary and compensation must be an appropriate and fair exchange of value. The compensation must be commensurate with the amount of (and value of) work being done, and it must be distributed from a place of gratitude for work well done.

For example, I was working with an organization that had instituted an incentive bonus program. The bonus program was well established and had been carefully designed. A bonus was distributed when (and only when) there was an increase in profit margin for the company based on predetermined criteria. The organization's financial advisors and management team had developed the plan, and the owner was fully committed and in agreement. The plan was based on the premise that a bonus had to be good for the organization, good for the owner and shareholders, and good for the team members. A bonus could not—and would not—be distributed unless those predetermined criteria were met.

It came to pass that one month, the team was eligible for a bonus. When the owner came to the team with the bonus checks, he slammed them down on the conference table at a team meeting and said, "I hope you are happy with these checks. They cost me an arm and a leg."

Well, that was not exactly true. He still had both arms and both legs. And the bonus plan had been so carefully developed that the team could not make more money unless he did too.

The point of this example is that the team didn't want the money. Something they had worked diligently and enthusiastically toward had literally been thrown in their faces. The money was well deserved and fairly earned, but they didn't want it. It was dirty money. (They took it, of course.) From that point forward, the reason and the motivation behind that bonus program was corrupt. It no longer worked, and it was disassembled.

Don't start something if you are not fully committed to implementing it with dedication and enthusiasm. Your false acceptance of the program will ultimately cause it to fail. That's why careful analysis and structuring is of vital importance to this very personal and emotional issue. Money is a very personal part of a person's life and needs to be handled with care.

Salary or bonus—or any monetary reward—is a motivator when the employer

- gives the paycheck to the employee with gratefulness
- gives an increase in salary in direct relationship to achievement of goals reached or the addition of responsibilities
- properly aligns the reward with performance
- recognizes performance over and above expectation (Herzberg, 1966)
- accesses the support and consultation of experts in the field of compensation, when and where desirable and possible
- uses a fair and equitable evaluation of performance responsibilities and accomplishments, as well as norms in your industry
- is fair and equitable and the reward falls into the range of possibility in your budget and in your corporate structure

- accurately determines equitability with clear goals and expectations that have been agreed upon and met

Guessing and hoping are not rational methods of determining salary and compensation. It takes better systems, planning, and communication than that. Measurement is essential.

Herzberg also determined that salary became a "dissatisfier" or demotivator when

- salary or bonuses were not fair and equitable
- money was offered as a carrot (trying to get a person to do a good job if they weren't doing so at that time)

Trying to get people to perform better because you are going to give them more money will not necessarily improve output or quality. These people will gripe about money no matter what. They are the *carping skeptics* and won't often change their behaviors, attitudes, or mind-sets when money is held out as a carrot.

Be grateful for what you have and stop complaining—it bores everybody else, does you no good, and doesn't solve any problems.
—Zig Ziglar

However, people who are entrepreneurs, drivers, or engaged members of team can be motivated and are grateful for appropriate rewards for work well done. Leaders are challenged to match the compensation of employees to the individual needs and desires of that employee. *Creating a Healthy Work Environment* recommends establishing and maintaining equitable compensation for employees, resulting in equitable growth and stability for organizations.

Creative Opportunities

1. Identify methods of compensation that are motivational and important to team members.
2. Identify methods of compensation that are motivational and important to the executive team and the vitality of the organization.
3. How can there be a congenial and equitable melding of these two areas of need?
4. If there are to be increases in salary or compensation to employees, how could those increases be determined so that the health of the organization is not compromised?
5. How could team members earn their own increases in salary by helping increase the revenues of the company?
6. What are the personal benefits of this to the employees? What are the financial benefits?

CHAPTER 24

Change

Life is filled with changes. *It's whether we can cope with those changes or not that determines whether we will grow with the situation or be overcome by it, whether we will act helplessly or have hope.*
-----Joan Borysenko, PhD

To accept change, employees and team members must mentally and emotionally believe in the change—and in the leaders who are instituting the change. Change is inevitable. Change is considered an essential element of relevancy in any profession or industry. The day an organization decides to stay the same (or thinks it is as good as it can get) is the day it decides to go downhill. If you decide to remain the same, the rest of the world will pass you by. That is true of any aspect of our lives.

Having said that, many principles of life and of work discussed in this book do not change, including the characteristics of a person that are foundational, meaningful, and good: integrity, respect, trust, and commitment. The foundation of an honorable company is based on solid principles: principles that define who they are, what they do, and how they do it. If the foundation is solid and unwavering, decisions or actions will exemplify that foundation (the principles upon which it stands).

Change as an Asset of Growth

At times, change is desirable and necessary. However, it is not always easy to change. Some people dig in their heels and balk at the suggestion of change. By looking at change from a progressive perspective, it can become your friend.

Willingness to change begins in the mind, and when people decide not to change, that decision can be a roadblock. There are numerous reasons people resist change. A few of these reasons are listed here, but you may think of many others.

- Previous changes may not have produced desired results.
- The team may not have been included in the decision to change.
- The change may have been thrown at the team as a mandate without any preparation or involvement in the process itself.
- Things may have been done a certain way for so long that change seems unnecessary.
- Adequate skill level may be absent.

People may sabotage a change idea because they don't want to look inadequate (not because the idea is poor). They negate the idea instead of admitting the need for further education or change in themselves (Bennis and Nanus, 1997).

When leaders accept responsibility to *influence* their teams, change can happen. Inspirational leaders can generate a sense of trust and faith in ideas that may seem impossible or far-reaching but, in fact, are reachable (Kotter and Cohen, 2002). Stagnant thinking can be an enormous barrier to progress. However, with effective leadership, the generative mind can become a company's greatest asset. If people are going to be prepared for and execute dynamic change, leaders must engage in constant communication about the vision and stress to employees how that change will benefit them and the customers (Kotter, 1996).

Helping People Change

Change is an inevitable part of a growing, progressive business, but it is not always greeted with open arms. Resistance to change is not unusual. Most agents of change realize they can better assist other people toward effective, independent functioning by helping people help themselves. *Independent functioning* means team members are motivated to implement changes and maintain the new ways without dropping back to the old ways. For independent functioning to occur, these five factors need to be in place:

- leaders who are enthusiastic about change
- clear vision of the benefits of the proposed change and the effects of the change on individual team members and on the organization as a whole
- a distinct plan of action
- instruction for any newly required skills
- encouragement (Kanfer and Goldstein, 1991)

Dr. Charles Puntillo of Burlington, Wisconsin, is an owner of a successful small business who understands the value of helping his team members accept change.

> Our business is constantly in a dynamic state. It is a challenge that we accept. I've tried to create an environment where change is not only accepted, but where people are excited by it rather than afraid of it. Even if there is great apprehension, if we believe the change will be beneficial, we go for it. Then, we celebrate the success. That success motivates us to search for new and better ways of doing things.
>
> If we are not willing to change, everything will pass us by. We may feel that we are on the "cutting edge" but if we become complacent and think that

> we have "arrived," that thought process becomes detrimental. Commitment to change and progress has to be burning within the owner/CEO before team members enthusiastically embrace change. If the leader is wishy-washy about a change, that sends a mixed signal to the rest of the organization. They may think that "status quo" is OK. When you, as the leader, have to make decisions, get committed to those decisions and don't falter. The team will stand behind firm decisions that are backed up with reason and validation.

Dr. Larry Rosenthal of New York City adds, "Change is absolutely inevitable—whether we want to admit it or not."

Change: The System

"What? You even recommend a system for the change process?" Absolutely, I do. Without a carefully developed system, changes that are desired in the workplace may not occur. The organization risks falling behind, stagnating, and losing market share. A carefully developed system that works well will help you through the large and small changes that are crucial and desirable.

Consider the system I am going to recommend. It works, and it works well. Tweak it where you feel appropriate, but it has a proven track record based on research and history. You will find change to be less threatening and more readily accepted.

Decide if the change you are initiating is necessary, valuable, or beneficial. This short checklist can help you determine if the change is appropriate.

A Change Checklist

Yes No

____ ____ Is this change compatible with the purpose and mission of the organization?

____ ____ Will this change benefit the team members? Will it benefit the organization?

____ ____ Is the reason for this change specific and clear? Are the leaders and the team members informed?

When you study the reasons people resist change, you will recognize these. You can list many situations or circumstances where you faced these issues. The reason behind the resistance may change from situation to situation and from person to person. Find out which of these are applicable to your situation and face these issues "head-on."

1. The change isn't self-initiated.
2. People's routines are disrupted.
3. It creates fear of the unknown.
4. The purpose of the change is unknown.
5. It creates a fear of failure.
6. The rewards don't match the required effort.
7. Too satisfied with the status quo.
8. People engage in negative thinking or negative talk.
9. The followers lack respect for the leader.

10. The leader is susceptible to feelings of personal criticism.
11. It creates fear of personal loss.
12. It requires additional commitment.
13. Narrow-mindedness thwarts acceptance of new ideas.
14. Tradition resists change.

If you have people who are mostly supportive of change, once they understand it and see the benefits of it, that's great. You may have one person or one division where resistance is constant. Do everything you can to help someone be successful. If there is no willingness on the part of a team member to alter when essential, a change of position or a change of employment may be necessary.

You will recognize this familiar "diffusion of innovations" graph—or Rogers's bell curve. This curve illustrates how people buy and how people change!

We all can recognize customers and clients who fit into each area of this graph. Of course, you can identify people in your own organization who range from innovator to laggard. The way you approach, teach, and handle each person is unique. Individualize your presentation and your efforts to get full commitment. Remember that there are multiple leaders in an organization. Identify the leaders in a division or department and get them on board first. They will be your advocates—your innovators. Their enthusiasm will influence other people in their departments. If you fail to get the innovators "with you," your chances of moving through a change process could be difficult (if not impossible).

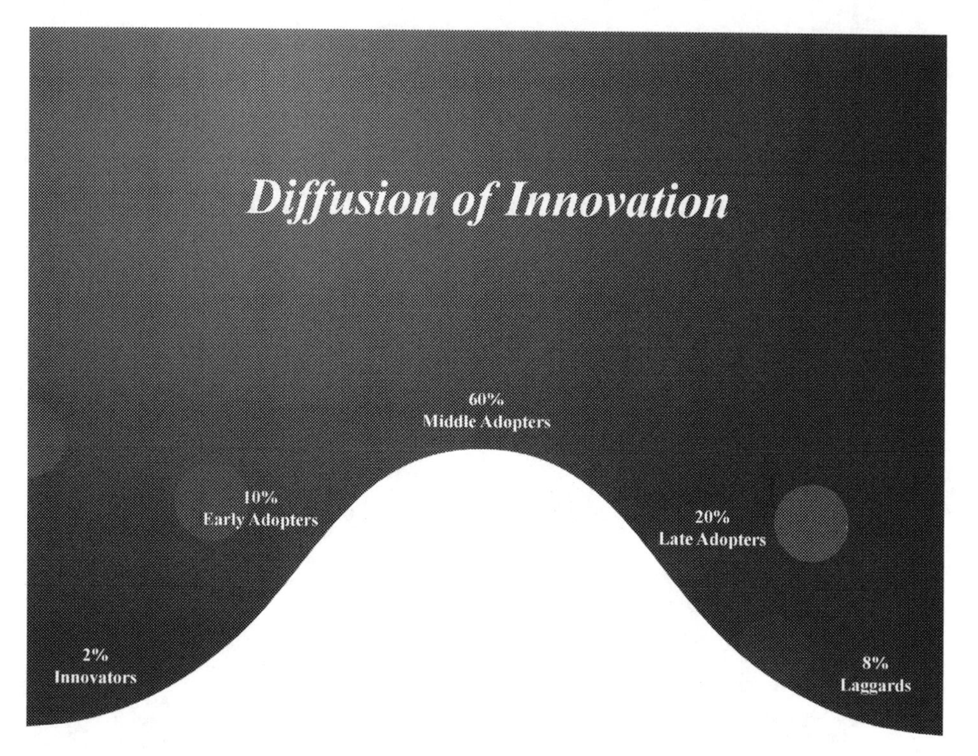

Rogers's Bell Curve

Now start your campaign. Here are the details of how to organize and influence change. It looks tedious because I have broken it down into bite-sized pieces, but once you get the system into place and start using this system, it will fit into almost everything you do. It will become second nature. The system will help you bring new products, services, or processes into your environment or your market. Once people get used to the new ways and see the benefits, they will not go back to the old ways—even if they could. You want people to "own" the changes.

Ten-Step Process or System for Implementing Change

1. Inform people in advance of the impending changes. Speak with your innovators first. Get the innovators on your side. Help them see the benefits and get excited. Then introduce the change to the remainder of the team—or whoever will be impacted by the change.
2. Explain the "why." Why is this being presented, suggested, or required? Why is an alternative or a new way necessary or desired? Remember that people are motivated by the "why," not the "what."
3. Describe the benefits of the change to the individuals, divisions, clients, and the organization as a whole. In other words, whoever will be affected.
4. Ask them (invite them) to participate. Ask for their support. Ask them to be innovators and leaders.
5. Keep the clear channels of communication open. Be ready to handle the difficulties and the challenges. If you are sincere about instituting a change, do not back away from it just because you get resistance. Stand firm—but be compassionate and listen.
6. Be flexible and adaptable. If you have set a goal to implement a change and have designed a plan of action, but healthy outcomes are not happening, evaluate. "Is this something we really want to do?" If the answer is yes, go back to the plan and restructure it. Keep on doing the things that are working and alter the things that are not. Be flexible, but do not quit.
7. Show enthusiasm for the project or innovation. Be committed. Be consistent. Show how strongly you believe in the purpose of the innovation.
8. Be enthusiastic. Remember that you cannot buy enthusiasm—but you can catch it. Let your people catch your enthusiasm.

9. Be supportive of people during the change process. Hold hands when necessary (figuratively speaking, of course). Adjust when necessary. Give praise when appropriate.
10. Celebrate the victories along the way! Provide recognition for work well done. Express your confidence and pride in the people who are moving toward that change. Give feedback on progress and provide regular updates on results.

As a leader, be out front to encourage change and growth. Don't let yourself get stuck in old ways. Be a change maker. Show the way. Be an example.

When you're through changing, you're through.
—John Maxwell

As you work toward creating a healthy work environment, you will go through changes. Be prepared. You can do it. Take things one step at a time. Recognize each step and be grateful for the movement forward. When you express sincere gratitude and appreciation along the path, people will respond with returned support and faithful effort.

Creative Opportunities

1. Identify one change that you (or the team) believe would be valuable, beneficial, and productive.
2. Using the checklist in this chapter, ask those questions. Discuss the answers that are offered.
3. If you decide that the change would be beneficial, go through the ten-step process. Determine who you need to "get on board" and how you will do that.
4. Discuss the reasons people resist change. Do you recognize any of these in your coworkers? In yourself? How can you

carefully and caringly get these "late adopters" or "laggards" (I wouldn't actually call them that!) on board?

5. Use the five-step goal-accomplishment form from chapter 10 to design a plan of action from top to bottom. Evaluate along the path. Be flexible and adjust when necessary.
6. The change may be a big one for a person who is cautious or uncomfortable with change. Celebrate each step that someone takes down a forward path.

CHAPTER 25

Reflections and Telescopes

People's work is an important part of their total life.
When people enjoy and find a sense of purpose in
their work, they discover that elusive fulfillment that
is being sought by people in the workplace today.
—Dr. Cathy Jameson

You have read, studied, and reflected on the elements of creating a healthy work environment. I hope you see the benefits to yourself, your teammates, and your organization. There is work to be done on each person's part as each individual accepts his or her role as a leader: leader of self, leader of teammates, and leader of clients.

You may be wondering how to put the concepts into action. I have tried to follow the concepts of adult learning in this book so that this will be more than a book to read and put on the shelf. I hope it will serve as a guideline for your continuous progress and development, including the following:

- theory and research to support the validity of each concept and recommendation
- examples to illustrate how those concepts and recommendations can work in reality
- steps for how to proceed
- action items (creative opportunities) that bring the material to life for you and your organization

Now let me reflect on some of the key points that will be of value to you as you move forward. Let these final thoughts be motivational as you take your first steps! Your successes will motivate you to take the next step—and so on. The path is wide open for you. Take that first step.

Faith is taking the first step even when you don't see the whole staircase.
—Dr. Martin Luther King Jr.

Key Points

- Be a visionary. Look into the future. Focus.
- A healthy work environment is built on excellent teamwork, support, friendships, unified spirit, pride, and commitment to clients and teammates. When people feel their contributions are valuable and significant parts of the success of the company, they will deliver on work requirements in a more passionate and energetic manner.
- Although it is essential that a company get and maintain a positive profit margin, paying attention to the money and not to the people will cost a company if quality people leave.
- People want independence, trust, respect, and dignity. The knowledge worker today is interested in and capable of

participating in company decisions. This participation will not take away from work capacity; it will build on it because of the increased energy resulting from recognition and acknowledgement of employees' intellectual and leadership capabilities.

- A great team is a group of leaders working cohesively toward a common set of goals. A sense of co-ownership of the organization results when people on the team believe in and support the vision of the "ideal" and realize that the vision belongs to everyone (Jameson, 2010).
- People can and will leap into executing projects when they are clear about the vision—the "why." Supporting the progress and expressions of appreciation along the path will lead to energized performance and fulfilled results.
- When talented people are challenged and encouraged, performance usually accelerates. Clear goals and expectations related to performance become the guideline for progress.

Team members of The Jameson Group

- In a work environment where the mode of operation is support and education (rather than reprimands and confusion), people's self-esteem is elevated. The result is internal confidence that translates to good work and good results.
- Be fruitful to the souls of the people who work with you. When you build up people instead of tearing them down, you nurture the innermost part of their being (the soul). Work without soulfulness is empty and meaningless. Work that comes from the depths of one's goodness is powerful beyond measure.
- *Creating a Healthy Work Environment* has one purpose: to teach, support, and nurture the brilliance, grace, and love of people in all walks of life, but certainly in the workplace. In a work environment that lives and breathes the principles we

have studied together, people find joy and happiness in work that is fulfilling.

- And then, people can accept the privilege of "giving".

My long-term client, colleague, coauthor, and beloved friend, Dr. Linda Greenwall, was raised in Cape Town, South Africa, and now lives in London. From the very first time she heard me speak, she said, "That's the way I want to manage my business." We have worked together to create a healthy work environment where she and her team members thrive. Love of clients, love of service, and love for each other is a reality. It is more than a lesson in a book; it is a daily reality.

I want to include a photo and a letter from Dr. Greenwall that speak of her belief in giving back. For her, for you, and for me, *Creating a Healthy Work Environment* gives us the privilege of sharing our abundance with others and making a difference.

Giving Back

At a time in your career and professional development, you may wish to reflect on all the wonderful opportunities that have come your way to enable you to be the person that you now are. Gratitude is attitude! You may want to show your gratitude by giving back in some way to society, your community, or your profession. When I reached a milestone birthday, instead of thinking about it, I decided to do something about it. I started a charity, the Dental Wellness Trust www.dentalwellnesstrust.org. Being a dentist for thirty years, I decided to give back in the form of teaching oral health to vulnerable kids, street kids, and orphans. After three years, we are now working with ten thousand children in the townships of South Africa, and we have undertaken projects in the UK, Ghana, Rwanda, South Africa, Croatia, and other countries. I have found that it has been a joy to give back—and that one gets more out of it than one gives. It has changed my life.

Thank you, Cathy, for inspiring me to be the best that I can be!
https://www.youtube.com/user/DentalWellnessTrust
Best wishes,
Dr. Linda Greenwall

Dental
Trust
love
you

CHAPTER 26

Fun!

I believe we create our own life. And we create it by our own belief system. I think we are born with this huge canvas in front of us and the paintbrushes and the paint. We choose what to put on this canvas.
—Louise L. Hay

Fun

I think life should and can be fun—enjoyable! How about you? Work can be a part of a fun-filled life. Work can be enjoyable—and so can the people in the workplace.

Of course there are serious moments in every life, and not all experiences are fun. However, every aspect of life is part of a complete, comprehensive life. Make efforts to gain wisdom and insight from the joyful times and the tragic times, from the delightful moments and the painful moments, from the carefree days and the stress-filled days. A fulfilled life is not seamless; it is one that has been finely crafted by weaving together all aspects of life experiences to complete and fulfill us. The people who gain peace from well-lived lives are those who discover the wisdom that comes from being present in each and every moment—and learning from each. If you commit to living in a place of gratitude, grace, and love, fun can be part of every aspect of your life.

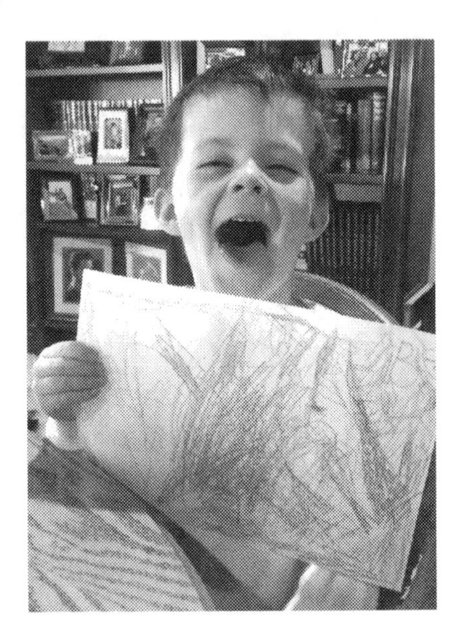

Our Grandson, Ben, painting on his young canvas of life!

Sharing this book with you has been fun. Certainly, there has been much work, diligent effort, challenges, joys, and constant communication with many people. I have loved the process and the sharing. Therefore, my work has been fun.

I have loved connecting with you. Let's stay connected. After all, relationships and connectedness mean everything in the span of a lifetime. Join me on my blog, cathyjameson.com. I will continue to share insights with you—and I look forward to hearing about your insights and experiences. Let's agree to fill our worlds with constructive communication and connectedness.

The following quote from Emerson reappeared to me during a recent trip to South Africa where I was lecturing and working with people from around the world who were doing wonderful things for humanity. Their lives and their work proved to be inspiring and motivational to me. Then this quote and I came face-to-face with one another. Although I have been familiar with this quote for years, it seemed to mean more upon this reading.

> To laugh often and much; to win the respect of intelligent people and the affection of children; to earn the appreciation of honest critics and endure the betrayal of false friends; to appreciate beauty, to find the best in others; to leave the world a bit better, whether by a healthy child, a garden, a redeemed social condition; to know even one life has breathed easier because you have lived. This is to have succeeded.
> —Ralph Waldo Emerson

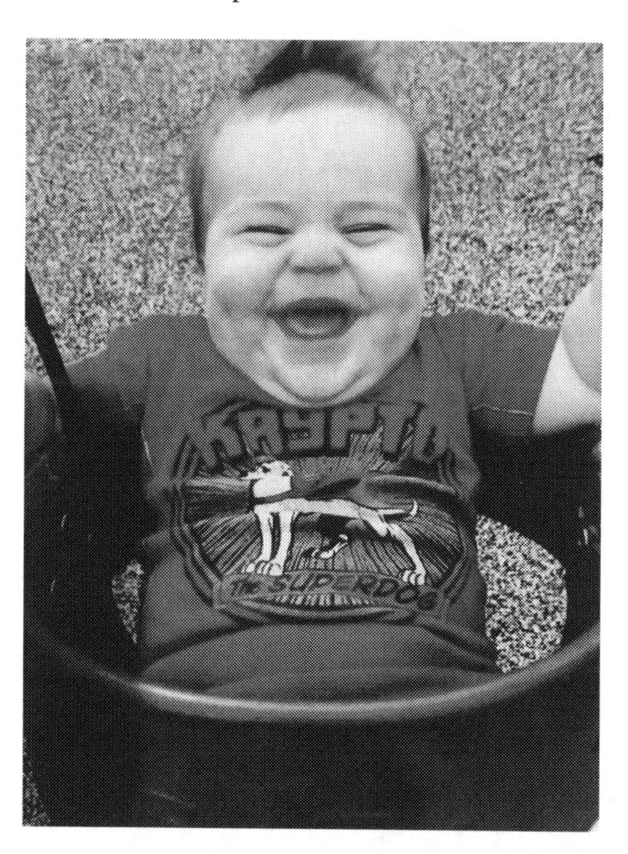

This photo of our grandson, Keller, says it all! I don't know about you, but I cannot see this photo and not break into a grin. Is there anything more joyful than hearing the laughter of an infant? This magnetic laughter is so natural and so much a part of the makeup of a new child. A baby finds such happiness in the simplest and most precious interactions of life: seeing his mommy come into the room, romping with his big brother, touching the hair of a cat or dog, being held by the strong arms of his daddy, or swinging for the first time. The laughter is contagious because that type of simple joy and the ability to respond to it remains within us—even as we become seasoned adults.

Do we have to lose our joy in the workplace? I think not! That's what this book has been all about—as has been my life's work. Let's create healthy work environments where people can thrive, be happy, find fulfillment, and contribute to the world in positive, constructive ways.

It's okay to laugh at ourselves and laugh with others. We take ourselves so seriously. Every once in a while, relax. Laugh. There is nothing that is more therapeutic than a deep belly laugh. Remember to laugh with others—and not at them. Laugh with your own self—and rejoice in your own humanity.

Find the joys in every day—the simple wonderful things that bring a smile to your face. Then let yourself laugh. Laugh with pleasure—just because.

Believe in yourself and in your ability to expand your horizons. Fulfill the call of your chosen life's work. You can be all—or more—than you ever dreamed possible. Create a healthy work environment right where you are! Imagine the possibilities. Believe that these can become a reality and you will be well on your way.

—Cathy Jameson

Imagine

By

Cathy Jameson, PhD

Imagine.
Oh, the possibilities!
Endless.
That which the eye cannot see—but the mind can envision.
Think. Believe. Manifest.
Imagine.
Oh, the possibilities.
Timeless.
What others see as impossible—visualize as real.
Ideas. Innovation. Uniqueness.
Imagine.
Oh, the possibilities.
Potential realized.
Using your gifts and talents to create health and happiness for another.
Create. Step out of the norm. Persevere with passion.
Imagine.
Oh, the possibilities,
Miracles fulfilled.
Acknowledge, explore, maximize talent. Go beyond the expected, the easy, the ordinary.
Be spectacular. Make a difference. Be on purpose. Unwrap your gift from God—your unique self—and move toward God's dream for you.
Imagine.

BIBLIOGRAPHY

Anderson, C. R. (1988). *Management: Skills, Functions, and Organization Performance* (2nd ed.). Boston, MA: Allyn and Bacon.

Anderson, N. (2013, January 3). *5 ways to make your new year's resolutions stick.* Retrieved from http://www.forbes.com/sites/financialfinesse/2013/01/03/5-ways-to-make-your-new-years-resolutions-stick.

Bass, B. M., and Avolio. B. J. (1994). Improving organizational effectiveness through transformational leadership. Thousand Oaks, CA: Sage.

Belasco, J. (1991). *Teaching the Elephant to Dance: The Manager's Guide to Empowering Change.* New York, NY: Plume.

Bennis, W., and Nanus, B. (1997). *Leaders: The strategies of taking charge.* New York, NY: Harper and Row.

Bennis, W., and Townsend, R. (2005). *Reinventing leadership.* New York, NY: HarperCollins.

Blanchard, K. (1993). *Raving fans.* New York, NY: William Morrow.

Blanchard, K. (2000). *The one minute manager builds high performing teams.* New York, NY: Harper-Collins.

Booth, H. N. (1997). *Thriving on change.* San Diego, CA: Harrison Acorn Press.

Bossidy, L., and Charan. R. (2002). *Execution. The discipline of getting things done.* New York, NY: Crown Business.

Cameron, J. (2002). *The artist's way.* New York, NY: Tarcher/Putnam.

Carroll, R. (2015). What is a business system [Web log]. The System Thinker Blog. Retrieved from Box Theory Business Systems.

Chaney, S. (2004). Six best and worst incentives for professional development. *Delta, 70*(2), 10–14.

Charan, R., and Bossidy, L. (2002). *Execution.* New York, NY: Crown.

Cohen, S. (2006). Compliment your staff with nonmonetary rewards. *Nursing Management, 37*(12), 10–14.

Collins, J. (2001). *Good to great.* New York, NY: HarperCollins.

Covey, S. (1989). *7 habits of highly effective people.* New York, NY: Free Press.

Covey, S. (1992). *Principle-centered leadership.* New York, NY: Summit Books.

Covey, S., and Merrill, R. R. (2006). *The speed of trust.* New York, NY: Free Press.

Coy, D., and Kovacs-Long, J. (2005). Maslow and Miller: An exploration of gender and affiliation in the journey to competence. *Journal of Counseling and Development, 83,* 138–145. doi:10.1002/j.1556-6678.2005.tb00590.x

Csikszentmihalyi, M. (1990). *Flow: The psychology of optimal experience.* New York, NY: Harper and Row.

Csikszentmihalyi, M., Rathunde, K., and Whalen, S. (1993). *Talented teenagers: The roots of success and failure.* New York, NY: Cambridge University Press.

Decision making. (2015). *Business Dictionary.* Retrieved from http://www.businessdictionary.com/definition/decision-making.html

Deming, W. E. (1982). *Out of crisis.* Cambridge, MA: MIT Press.

DePree, M. (1989). *Leadership is an art.* New York, NY: Bantam Doubleday Dell.

Dispenza, J. (2013). *Breaking the habit of being yourself: How to lose your mind and find a new one.* Carlsbad, CA: Hay House.

Drucker, P. (1999). *Management challenges for the 21st century.* New York, NY: HarperCollins.

Drucker, P. (2002). *The effective executive.* New York, NY: Harper-Collins.

Durkheim, E. (1961). *Moral education.* New York, NY: The Free Press.

Dyer, W. (1976). *Your erroneous zones.* New York, NY: HarperCollins.

Emmons, R. (2010). *Why gratitude is good.* Retrieved from http://greatergood.berkeley.edu/article/item/why gratitude_is_good

Fernando, A. (2006). Why punish, when you can reward? Online or off-line, there are simple steps you can take to make your customers feel valued. *Communication World Magazine, 9,* 14–15.

Foreman, E. (2014). *Laughing, loving, and living.* Wheeling, IL: Nightingale-Conant.

Frankl, V., and Winslade, W. J. (2014). *Man's search for meaning.* Boston, MA: Beacon Press.

Gerber, M. (1990). *The E-myth.* New York, NY: Harper Business.

Gordon, T. (2009). *Leader effectiveness training.* New York, NY: Peter H. Wyden.

Greasley, D., and Madsen, J. (2006). Employee and total factor productivity convergence. *KYKLOS, 59,* 527–555. doi:10.1111/j.1467-6435.2006.00348.x

Greenwall, L., and Jameson, C. (2012). *Success strategies for the aesthetic dental practice.* Berlin, Germany: Quintessence.

Harris, K., and Kacmar, K. (2006). Too much of a good thing. The curvilinear effect of leader–member exchange on stress. *The Journal of Social Psychology, 146,* 65–84. doi:10.3200/SOCP.146.1.65-84

Hartline, M., and Ferrell, O. C. (1996). The management of customer-contact service employees: An empirical investigation. *Journal of Marketing, 60*(4), 52–62. doi:10.2307/1251901

Herman, R. E. (1999). Keeping good people. Winchester, VA: Oakhill Press.

Herzberg, F. (1966). *Work and the nature of man.* Cleveland, OH: World.

Herzberg, F. (2003). One more time: How do you motivate employees? *Harvard Business Review, 81,* 86–97.

Herzberg, F., Mausner, B., and Snyderman, B. B. (2007). *The motivation to work.* New York, NY: John Wiley and Sons.

Hill, N. (1966). *Think and grow rich.* North Hollywood, CA: Hal Leighton.

Hoffman, E. L. (Ed.). (1996). *The unpublished papers of Abraham Maslow.* Thousand Oaks, CA: Sage.

Houkes, I., Janssen, P., de Jonge, J., and Bakker, A. (2003). Specific determinants of intrinsic work motivation, emotional exhaustion and turnover intention: A multisample longitudinal study. *Journal of Occupational Psychology, 76,* 427–450. doi:10.1348/096317903322591578

Inkpen, A. (2005). Learning through alliances: General Motors and NUMMI. *California Management Review, 47*(4), 114–136. doi:10.2307/41166319

Ireland, D., and Hitt, M. A. (1992). Mission statements: Importance, challenge, and recommendations for development. *Business Horizons, 35*(3), 34–43. doi:10.1016/0007-6813(92)90067-J

James. M. B. (2013). *Conscious of the unconscious.* Retrieved from https://www.psychologytoday.com/blog/focus-forgiveness/201307/conscious-the-unconscious

Jameson, C. (2000). *Controlling stress in the dental profession through effective communication.* Oklahoma City, OK: JC Educational.

Jameson, C. (2004). *Great communication equals great production.* Tulsa, OK: Pennwell Books.

Jameson, C. (2007). *Leadership symposium.* Oklahoma City, OK: JC Educational.

Jameson, C. (2008). *KAM II* (Unpublished manuscript). Walden University, Minneapolis.

Jameson, C. (2010). *The impact of training in transformational leadership on the productivity of a dental practice* (Doctoral dissertation). Available from ProQuest Dissertations and Theses database. (UMI No. 3409492)

Joseph, S., and Linley, P. A. (2006). Positive psychology versus the medical model. *The American Psychologist, 61,* 332–333. doi:10.1037/0003-066X.60.4.332

Joshua-Amadi, M. (2002). Recruitment and retention. *Nursing Management, 9*(8), 17–21. doi:10.7748/nm2002.12.9.8.17.c2134

Kanfer, F. H., and Goldstein, A. P. (1991). *Helping people change.* Boston, MA: Allyn and Bacon.

Kashefi, M. (2007). Work flexibility and its individual consequences. *Canadian Journal of Sociology, 32,* 341–369. doi:10.2307/20460647

Kotter, J. (1996). *Leading change.* Boston, MA: Harvard Business School Press.

Kotter, J. (2008). *A sense of urgency.* Boston, MA: Harvard Business School Press.

Kotter, J., and Cohen, D. (2002). *The heart of change.* Boston, MA: Harvard Business School Press.

LeBoeuf, M. (1985). *The GMP: The greatest management principle in the world.* New York, NY: Putnam.

LeBoeuf, M. (1989). *Getting results.* New York, NY: Berkeley Books.

Leider, R. (1997). *The power of purpose.* Emeryville, CA: Berrett-Koehler.

Lindahl, L. (1949). What makes a good job? *Personnel, 25,* 263–266.

Martin, C. (2005). Leadership: Make it h.o.t. *Nursing Management, 36*(9), 38–45. doi:10.1097/00006247-200509000-00010

Maslow, A. (1965). *Eupsychian management.* Homewood, IL: Richard Invin and Dorsey Press.

Maslow, A. (1971). *The farther reaches of human nature.* New York, NY: The Viking Press.

Maslow, A. (1987). *Motivation and personality.* New York, NY: Addison-Wesley Educational.

Maslow, A. (1998). *Maslow on management.* New York, NY: John Wiley and Sons.

Maslow, A. (1999). *Toward a psychology of being.* New York, NY: John Wiley and Sons.

Maslow, A. (2000). *The Maslow business reader.* New York, NY: John Wiley and Sons.

Mayo, E. (1932). *The Hawthorne effect.* Cicero, IL: Western Electric Works.

McClelland, D. (1989). *Human motivation.* New York, NY: Scott-Foreman.

McColl, P. (2007). *Your destiny switch: Master your key emotions, and attract the life of your dreams.* Carlsbad, CA: Hay House.

McKnight, D. H., Ahmad, S., and Schroeder, R. G. (2001). When do feedback, incentive control, and autonomy improve morale? The importance of employee-management relationship closeness. *Journal of Managerial Issues, 13,* 466–482. Retrieved from https://www.msu.edu/~mcknig26/Morale.pdf

McLagan, P. (2003). Secrets to organizational greatness. *Consulting to Management, 14*(1), 7–11.

Merton, T. (1949). *Social theory and social structure.* New York, NY: The Free Press.

Morin, A. (2014). *What mentally strong people don't do.* New York, NY: Harper-Collins.

Mullins, M. E., and Devendorf, S. A. (2007). Assessing goal-directed attention as an indicator of self-regulation: A comparison of two approaches. *North American Journal of Psychology, 9,* 229–250.

Murphy, K. (1987). *Effective listening.* New York, NY: Bantam Books.

Murphy, L. (2005). Transformational leadership: A cascading chain reaction. *Journal of Nursing Management, 13,* 128–136. doi:10.1111/j.1365-2934.2005.00458.x

Nightingale, E. (2013). *The strangest secret* (3rd ed.). Seaside, OR: Rough Draft.

Northrup, C. (2015). *Goddesses never age.* Carlsbad, CA: Hay House.

Pannunzio, C. (2011). *One thought on "the power of a powerful mission statement.* Retrieved from http://practicemanagementblog.onefpa.org/2010/07/19/the-power-of-a-powerful-mission-statement/

Peters, T., and Waterman, R. (1985). *In search of excellence.* New York, NY: Warner Books.

Phaneuf, M. (2005, February). *The mirror effect: Mediator of knowledge and self-image.* Paper presented at the conference of the Philosophy and Education Convention, Evora, Portugal. Retrieved from http://www.infiressources.ca/fer/Depotdocument_anglais/Mirror_Effect.pdf

Qubein, N. (1997). *How to be a great communicator.* New York, NY: John Wiley and Sons.

Rogers, E. (2003). *Diffusion of innovations.* (5th ed.). New York, NY: Free Press.

Schucman, H., and Thetford, W. (1996). *A course in miracles* (2nd ed.). New York, NY: Viking Penguin.

Scovel Shinn, F. (2012). *The new game of life and how to play it.* New York, NY: Atria Books.

Senge, P. (2006). *The fifth discipline.* New York, NY: Doubleday.

Senge, P., Scharmer, C., Jaworski, J., and Flowers, B. (2004). *Presence: Human purpose and the field of the future.* New York, NY: Doubleday.

Smilko, J., and Van Neck, K. (2004). Rewarding excellence through variable pay. *Benefits Quarterly, 20*(3), 21–25.

Strickler, J. (2006). What really motivates people? *Journal for Quality and Participation, 29*(1), 26–28.

Strumpfer, D. (2005). Standing on the shoulders of giants: Notes on early positive psychology (psychofortology). *South African Journal of Psychology, 35,* 21–45. doi:10.1177/008124630503500102

Sturkey, M. F. (2009). *Warrior culture of the U.S. Marines* (3rd ed.). Plum Branch, SC: Heritage Press International.

Swanwick, T. (2005). Organizational structure and culture in postgraduate general practice education: Implications for the management and leadership of change. *Education for Primary Care, 16,* 115–128.

Toftoy, C. N., and Chatterjee, J. (2014). The value of mission statements for small businesses. Washington, DC: George Washington University School of Business and Public Management, Department of Management Science.

Vaughan, F., Walsh, R., and Williamson, M. (Eds.). (1995). Gifts from a course in miracles. New York, NY: Jeremy P. Tarcher/Putnam.

Walton, M. (1990). *Deming at work.* New York, NY: Perigee Books.

Warren, R. (2002). *The purpose driven life.* Grand Rapids, MI: Thomas Nelson.

Waterman, A. S. (2004). Finding someone to be: Studies on the role of intrinsic motivation in identity formation. *Identity, 4,* 209–228. doi:10.1207/s1532706xld0403_1

Webb, K. (2007). Motivating peak performance: Leadership behaviors that stimulate employee motivation and performance. *Christian Higher Education, 6,* 53–71. doi:10.1080/15363750600932890

Webfinanceinc.com (2015). *Decision making.* Retrieved from http://www.webfinanceinc.com

Weinberg, H. (2005). The effective time-binder and Maslow's "self-actualizing person." *ETC: A Review of General Semantics, 62,* 313–317.

Ziglar, Z. (1991). *On selling.* Nashville, TN: Oliver-Nelson Books.

APPENDIX

New Employee Orientation Checklist

Date____________________

Employee__________________________________ Date of Employment_________________

WELCOME

	Date completed	Superv./Mgr. and Employee to Initial
Introduction to Staff		
Tour of Facility		
History of the Organization		
Explanation of Type of Services		
Emergency Exits		
Employee's Job as It Relates to Business and Team Members		
Importance of Teamwork		
Performance Expectations		
See continued list at the bottom		

PERSONNEL RECORDS AND FORMS

(Place completed forms in employee's personnel folder)

Employment Eligibility Verification I-9 (Form #202)		
Wage and Tax Statement W-2		
Form W-4		
Employment Agreement (Form #200)		
Employee History - Confidential (Form #204)		
Employee Acknowledgment (Form #203)		
Other		
Safety Training Session		

Employee to Read the Policy Manual		

Work Schedule		
Personal Time Off		
Leaving Premises		
Attendance and Punctuality		
Material Review		
Sales Process Start to finish		
Goldmine		

WAGES AND SALARIES

Pay Day and Pay Period		
How Pay Is Figured		
Incentive Plan (*If applicable*)		
Wages and Salaries		
Payroll Dates		
Paid Holidays		
Payroll Deductions (Insurance, Taxes, etc.)		

EMPLOYMENT PRACTICES

	Date Completed	Superv./Mgr. and Employee to Initial
Terms of At-Will Employment		
Sexual Harassment		
Performance Review		
Problems Resolution Procedure		

EMPLOYEE BENEFITS

Benefits Chart		
Medical Benefits Program		
Leave of Absence		
Vacation Benefits		
Vacation Approval		
Holidays Falling During Vacation		
Paid Holidays		
Holidays on a Regular Scheduled Day Off		
Request for a Leave of Absence		

POLICIES

	Date Completed	Superv./Mgr. and Employee to Initial
Health and Safety		
Accidents or Injuries		
Appearance		
Personal Data Changes		
Parking		
Property or Equipment		
Office Security		
Personal Telephone Calls		
Confidentiality and Nondisclosure		

EMPLOYEE RELATIONS

	Date Completed	Superv./Mgr. and Employee to Initial
Responsibility and Conduct		
Unprofessional Conduct		

PERSONNEL POLICY MANUAL

Review		

JOB DESCRIPTION

Review the Written Job Descriptions		

PERFORMANCE REVIEWS

Review at Approx. 4 Weeks		
Review at 11 Weeks		

Comments: ____

____

____

____

Employee's signature ______________________________ **Date** ______________

cc: Employee's Personnel File

ABOUT THE AUTHOR

Cathy Jameson, PhD, and her husband, John H. Jameson, DDS, live on their family ranch, where they share their love for the land and American quarter horses with their beloved family.

Cathy founded an international management consulting firm and lectures, teaches, consults, and writes for organizations throughout the United States and the world. The subject of this book is the subject of her life's work.

Dr. Jameson holds a bachelor's degree in education, a master's degree in psychology, and a doctorate in applied management and decision sciences from Walden University. The focus of her study and research was transformational leadership and organizational change.

Dr. Jameson has been honored as a Hall of Fame recipient of the Oklahoma State University (OSU) College of Education and as a distinguished alumna of OSU. There she serves on the board of governors and has served on the board of trustees for the OSU Foundation. She has held adjunct faculty positions at major universities.

She provides motivational and instructional programs and keynotes for educational groups, universities, organizations, and corporations. She is a long-standing member of the National Speaker's Association and was a finalist for the Stevie Award for entrepreneurial women. Dr. Jameson has been named as one of the top twenty-five women in dentistry.

For further information about Cathy's products, seminars, keynotes, personal leadership coaching, or her blog, contact her via her website, www.cathyjameson.com.

For information about management consulting services, contact www.jamesonmanagement.com.

Cathy's Family

Printed in the United States
By Bookmasters